APPRAISING PRIMARY HEADTEACHERS

APPRAISING PRIMARY HEADTEACHERS

Challenge, confidence and clarity

*Eric Hewton and
Neville West*

Open University Press
Buckingham · Philadelphia

Open University Press
Celtic Court
22 Ballmoor
Buckingham
MK18 1XW

and
1900 Frost Road, Suite 101
Bristol, PA 19007, USA

First Published 1992

British Library Cataloguing-in-Publication Data

Hewton, Eric
  Appraising primary headteachers.
  I. Title   II. West, Neville
  371.1

  ISBN 0-335-09895-9

Library of Congress Cataloging-in-Publication Data

Hewton, Eric.
    Appraising primary headteachers: challenge, confidence, and
  clarity/Eric Hewton, Neville West.
      p.   cm.
    Includes bibliographical references (p.   ) and index.
    ISBN 0-335-09895-9
    1. Elementary school principals–Great Britain–Rating of.
  I. West, Neville.   II. Title.
  LB2831.662.H48   1991
  372.12'012'0941–dc20   91-21243
                                                   CIP

Typeset by Inforum Typesetting, Portsmouth
Printed in Great Britain by St Edmundsbury Press
Bury St Edmunds, Suffolk

Contents

_____ *Preface*

Background

Appraisal has not had a smooth passage since it was first mooted by Sir Keith Joseph almost a decade ago. It was sometimes referred to as 'teacher assessment' and was clearly associated with moves towards greater accountability and the never to be forgotten phrase, 'weeding out weak teachers'. As an issue, it became enmeshed with acrimonious negotiations over teachers' pay and conditions and in January 1986 the matter was referred to the Advisory, Conciliation and Arbitration Service (ACAS). A report by ACAS on appraisal and training was published in June of that year and this laid the foundation for a move forward towards a generally accepted form of 'developmental' appraisal.

Three Secretaries of State (Messrs Baker, MacGregor and Clarke) later, after a national pilot project involving six LEAs, an evaluation of the project by the Cambridge Institute of Education and a report by the National Steering Group (NSG) based at Bristol University, a Circular (12/91) and Regulations have now been published.

The NSG recommendations, with a few notable exceptions, have been accepted by the Government although it took some time for the different Secretaries of State to decide whether the scheme should be voluntary or compulsory. It was not until December 1990 that Mr Clarke informed the profession that he had decided upon the latter. In the coming few years LEAs, in different states of readiness, will attempt to introduce schemes that will comply with the Regulations.

In this they will be assisted by very limited funding (see pp. 56–7). The Government argues that appraisal simply brings together and formalizes good management practices that are, or should be, already implemented by schools. Exactly how LEAs and schools will cope in these circumstances during a time of increasing demands and strict financial auditing remains to be seen.

There is always the danger that if the time pressures associated with appraisal are felt to be too great by teachers and schools then a collusive exercise will take place. Appraisal will be carried out but with minimum effort, and will thereby produce minimum or even negative outcomes. This will be a great shame. There is much to be gained from appraisal and the messages from all the pilot authorities confirm this.

Headteacher appraisal

Within Circular 12/91 and the Regulations there are various references to headteacher appraisal. It is recognized that the process of appraisal involved will be different from that for teachers and could well be more expensive if done properly. A head has no easily identified line manager and it is not immediately clear who the appraiser(s) should be. The head also has a complex job involving responsibilities for several different areas of school's management. What should be appraised and to what depth are other difficult questions.

Because of these complexities, the pilot authorities and, from time to time, other schools and LEAs have tried various methods of headteacher appraisal, ranging from a panel of outsiders to a single colleague head from the same LEA. There have been a dozen or more approaches, each with its advantages and disadvantages.

The recommended approach, now endorsed by the Government, involves a headteacher appraiser from the same phase as the appraisee plus a representative from the LEA. Agreed aspects of the head's role will become the focus for appraisal during each two-year cycle. How schemes based upon these principles might be planned, the problems of implementing them and the ways in which such problems might be overcome are examined in detail in this book.

Our credentials

We are well placed to undertake the task of writing a book about primary headteacher appraisal. Both of us have been involved with several local authorities, almost from the start of the appraisal movement. We have worked closely with East Sussex, Croydon, Hampshire, Enfield and Jersey on teacher appraisal and more recently on the appraisal of heads and deputies in both the primary and secondary sector. Both of us have come to the problem with a background in educational management and a strong belief in appraisal as a form of staff development. We believed that the appraiser often gains as much from the process as the appraisee. We have both witnessed the positive outcomes of appraisal if properly handled but are convinced of the need for thorough training for appraisers and appraisees to ensure the success of any scheme.

Our experience has, however, been gained only with the help, co-operation and encouragement of the LEAs mentioned above and several hundred of their headteachers, to whom we express our gratitude. In particular we must thank Bob Garner and Barry Gooders of East Sussex and Robin Barnett and Roy Grigg, two headteachers who shared with us their thoughts and feelings about a real appraisal and agreed to write about it in Chapter 8. We would also like to acknowledge the contributions made by the many participants in workshops throughout the Country over the past five years. Finally, our thanks to the sterling efforts of Hayley Bloch, who battled her way through masses of drafts in record time and can still smile. Something surely to be commended at her next appraisal!

Eric Hewton
Neville West

1

The background to headteacher appraisal

In announcing his intention to introduce regulations for a national system of teacher and headteacher appraisal in December 1990, the Secretary of State for Education, Mr Kenneth Clarke, did no more than invoke the authority vested in him under the terms of the 1986 Education (No. 2) Act. But the idea of appraisal has been a live issue in the profession since the late 1970s and many advocates were disappointed when an earlier Secretary of State, Mr Kenneth Baker (1987–9), announced that he intended to defer its introduction. His successor, Mr John MacGregor (1989–90), relegated appraisal to voluntary status, a position now reversed by Kenneth Clarke.

There are many primary headteachers who hold the view that the earlier introduction of an effective appraisal system, rather than heavy emphasis on pupil assessment, would have greatly assisted them in their task of managing the changes brought about by the Education Reform Act and the introduction of the National Curriculum. Headteachers and their staff, working under pressure and often experiencing high levels of anxiety, could well have benefited from the kinds of recognition and support which should characterize an effective appraisal system. Appraisal would have soon identified that too much was being asked too quickly of headteachers, who are under contractual obligation to meet deadlines laid down in contemporary legislation. The Secretary of State has made clear his intentions and these are expressed in Regulations under Sections 49 and 63 of the Education (No. 2) Act.

The origins of the movement for a national system of appraisal are to be found in a range of sources stretching back to the early 1970s. The roots go deep and events along the way are many and varied. The debate has not been confined to the profession. Since 1973 there has been an expansion in the number of people who have a legitimate interest in the affairs of schools and how schools are managed by headteachers. Public awareness has been raised but there have been many instances where the press and media have conducted arguments based on simplistic ideas that reflect little understanding of the nature of teaching and learning and the complexities involved in running a school during a period of turbulence and change.

The purpose of this chapter is to provide a background to the issue of headteacher appraisal, to identify major influences which have informed debate on the subject and to outline the key points in two seminal documents: the ACAS report (ACAS, 1986a) and the report of the National Steering Group on teacher appraisal (NSG, 1989).

Three areas of discussion and debate have played a part in shaping decisions and influencing attitudes to the subject of appraisal:

- the concern for accountability, which emerged in the seventies;
- the self-evaluation and school improvement movement, which developed, in part, as a response to the call for improved standards;
- the focus on school management development, which accelerated after central government first identified management training for headteachers and senior staff as a priority in 1983.

Before we examine the reports specifically concerned with appraisal it will be helpful to consider certain perspectives and events in a little more detail.

The accountability movement

The demand for increased accountability was an expression of concern about standards in schools, teaching methods and spiralling costs set against the background of professional autonomy. Between 1969 and 1975 critics consistently attacked progressive methods adopted by primary schools in a series of what came to be called Black Papers (Cox *et al.*, 1969, 1970, 1975). Schools were felt to be insufficiently answerable to the clients they served. Events at William Tyndale School, described by Sallis (1977), illustrated the concerns aroused by the story of a school that appeared in the national media headlines.

Tyndale shocked everybody with the revelation that a whole generation of a school's children could suffer a terrifying slide into

demoralised chaos, while adults played pass-the-parcel with responsibility . . . The simple message of a very long report was that
nobody knew how to deal with it . . . There is no doubt that large
numbers of people who had never been concerned before got this
simple message.

(Sallis, 1977, p. 68)

Such events focused public attention on doubts about the condition of
education that were already being voiced in the press and by politicians. James Callaghan, the Labour Prime Minister, gave his Ruskin
speech in October 1976, in which he raised questions concerning levels
of accountability in the education service, standards in schools and the
nature of the curriculum. In his words, 'the educational system was out
of touch with the fundamental need for Britain to survive economi-
cally in a highly competitive world.'

The work of the Assessment and Performance Unit of the DES,
which was established in 1974 to gather data on pupil performance,
became more widely known. Primary headteachers were to find much
food for thought in the survey of primary schools carried out by HMI
between 1975 and 1977 and reported in Primary Education in England
(DES, 1978). Over two-thirds of the report was concerned with the
curriculum: its scope, content, the standards of pupil's work and con-
tinuity between age groups. It drew attention to shortcomings, particularly in relation to science, history and geography, and noted that
'it is disappointing to find that the great majority of teachers with posts
of special responsibility have little influence at present on the work of
other teachers.' Such comment fuelled discussion on levels of internal
and external accountability.

An attempt to examine accountability from a less overtly political
standpoint was made by a joint research project involving East Sussex
Education Authority, twenty-two primary schools and the University
of Sussex (Becher et al., 1981). It highlighted ways of improving
school–parent communications, introduced the notion of externally
audited school self-review (recently endorsed by several LEAs) and
drew attention to the importance of progress reviews for individual
pupils. Other researchers reached similar conclusions about the need
for more effective communications with parents, but their findings
made little impact and schools failed to stem a growing tide of parental
anxiety which, fanned by politicians and the media, opened the way
for the 1986 and 1988 Education Acts. The Sussex project also found
that many primary schools at that time (1977–9) still adhered to the
culture of 'zoned decision-making' (Lortie, 1975) whereby heads kept
out of the classroom while teachers kept out of school management.

This raised questions about heads' accountability to those outside the school for the quality of their internal systems of accountability involving all staff, which were in danger of being camouflaged by arguments about the uniqueness of schools and the proper nature of lay–professional relationships. The White Papers *Teaching Quality* (DES, 1983) and *Better Schools* (DES, 1985) called for more informed knowledge of teacher performance. *Better Schools* suggested the introduction of a system of teacher appraisal, which should seek to bring about:

- improved development and distribution of talent within the teaching force;
- help for all teachers (and by inference headteachers) to respond to changing demands, to realize their full professional potential by developing their strengths and improving weaknesses;
- identification of the most promising teachers for promotion;
- identification of those with professional difficulties and the provision of appropriate counselling, guidance and support;
- consideration for early retirement or dismissal of those teachers whose performance fails to improve to satisfactory levels after such guidance and support.

The 1985 White Paper also welcomed negotiations for a new salary structure and 'the introduction of systematic performance appraisal designed to bring about a better relationship between pay, responsibilities and performance' (para. 181), and went on, in relation to appraisal, to say

the Government believes that it may prove desirable or even necessary to provide that national framework in the form of statutory regulations . . . It is therefore proposed that the Secretary of State's existing powers for regulating the employment of teachers should be extended to enable him, in appropriate circumstances, to require LEAs regularly to appraise the performance of their teachers.

(DES, 1985, para. 183)

In this way a managerial and contractual accountability dimension to appraisal was asserted. *Better Schools* expresses a largely 'deficit' model of appraisal in which teachers are weighed and some found wanting. It is worth noting that appraisal became a central element in Burnham negotiations during 1985.

Quality in Schools: Evaluation and Appraisal (DES, 1985), produced by HMI, added impetus to the move towards systematic appraisal, noting that 'more attention needs to be given to the appraisal of middle managers in schools and even more to the appraisal of deputies and heads. For schemes to be effective they should include all staff and be seen to do so.' In the following year the 1986 Education (No. 2) Act sought to strengthen lines of accountability still further. The annual meeting of parents at which governors presented their report on the school was made a legal obligation and governors were given an equal voice in decisions relating to the appointment of staff.

The 1986 Education Act enabled LEAs to implement appraisal and established the basis for regulations which could be subsequently drawn upon in the regular appraisal of teachers 'discharging their duties' and 'engaging in activities connected with the establishments at which they are employed.' Although the 1986 pay settlement obliged teachers to take part in a national system of appraisal as part of their conditions of service it was made clear at that stage that appraisal was to be separated from issues relating to salary and promotion.

The spirit of accountability was clearly evident in the early documentation of Croydon's Pilot Appraisal Project (Croydon LEA, 1986), which stated:

> No useful or credible judgement can be made about a teacher's classroom effectiveness or performance without taking into account an assessment of the learning achieved by the teacher's pupils . . . Part of Croydon's appraisal scheme will therefore be concerned, in association with HAY-MSL with . . . seeking to relate their use (of Data Envelopment Analysis) to decision making, resource allocation, accountability and communication and information systems at school and local authority level in ways which achieve a closer and more direct managerial link between expenditure and the higher standards sought.
>
> (Croydon LEA, 1986, pp. 5–7)

As the Croydon pilot proceeded appraisal came to be located within a more developmental framework. However, for a time it still retained the notion that evidence of pupils' learning should be included in teacher appraisal provided it was properly contextualized.

The influence of accountability is also reflected in the *Report on the Evaluation of the School Teacher Appraisal Pilot Study* carried out by Cambridge Institute of Education (Bradley *et al.*, 1989). In their reference to headteacher appraisal the evaluators acknowledged that 'appraisal focuses attention on the headteacher role, and leads to a closer scrutiny of the head's contractual obligations than has been common in the past.' Accountability thus provides one rationale for appraisal but not one that would, in the form in which it was stated, easily engender full cooperation from the profession it was intended to serve.

Institutional self-evaluation and school improvement

Other influences that have informed the debate on appraisal are those which derive from the movement towards institutional self-evaluation and school improvement. After Tyndale (Auld, 1976) many LEAs produced frameworks for school review that primary headteachers might use in appraising their schools. An early example was *Keeping the School under Review* (ILEA, 1977). More recent examples of approaches to institutional evaluation are GRIDS (*Guidelines for Review and Internal Development in Schools*; McMahon *et al.*, 1984), *Setting Standards in Schools* (Steadman *et al.*, 1989) and *External Perspectives in School Based Review* (Abott *et al.*, 1989). All are aimed at assisting headteachers and their staff in engaging in the process of systematic school review.

Clift (1982) noted that

> by the middle of 1980 two thirds of LEAs in England and Wales had been involved in discussions on the topic of self-evaluation and about one fifth had produced agreed guidelines indicating to schools how they should go about evaluating themselves. All had produced guidelines suitable for primary schools.
>
> (pp. 262–3)

By 1985 the proportion had grown to four-fifths of the LEAs (Turner and Clift, 1985) and when the LEA pilot projects on appraisal commenced in 1987 *all* LEAs were supporting and developing systems for school self-evaluation. Alongside such initiatives and sharing similar concerns were the various projects which may be subsumed under the overarching title of 'school improvement'. An early exponent was the International Movement Towards Educational Change (IMTEC) founded under the auspices of the OECD, in which Dalin and Rust (1983) developed the Institutional Development Programme that aimed to 'facilitate effective school self-appraisal in British schools'. Another example was the International School Improvement Project, directed by a UK steering group and reported on by Hopkins (1987).

Concepts central to this school improvement movement have been developed by various projects and teams and have generally been well received by primary headteachers. Examples are the Developing School, outlined by Holly and Southworth (1989); the Self Managing School by Caldwell and Spinks (1988); the School Curriculum Initiative launched by Sheffield LEA (Clough *et al.*, 1989); and the School Focused Staff Development Project undertaken in East Sussex during the period 1985–7 (Hewton, 1988a). These and other initiatives adopted the notion of staff development interviews to identify the

development needs of individuals. The school improvement movement in the primary sector has also been fuelled by insights derived
from school-based research undertaken during the 1970s and 1980s.
Examples are King (1978), Galton *et al.* (1980), Bennett *et al.* (1984),
Rowland (1984), Alexander (1984), Mortimore *et al.* (1988) and Nias
et al. (1989). Each of these enquiries illuminates the complexity of
primary schools and identifies factors that should be borne in mind
when seeking to promote development. Most of them involved practising teachers in some way in the course of the research.

Each of these influences – self-evaluation, school improvement and
contemporary research – has the intention of enabling individual development *and* whole school development. They are committed to
notions of enablement and empowerment and share reflexive models
of learning which embrace teachers and pupils alike. Change is thus
accompanied 'by some re-thinking on the part of teachers about what
it means to learn' (Clough *et al.*, 1989).

Management development

A third influence on appraisal derives from a management development perspective that accelerated following Circular 3/83 from the
then Secretary of State, Keith Joseph. Many innovative programmes
primed by DES finance were established for headteachers and senior
staff in primary schools. Most programmes paid attention to the issue
of appraisal, its nature, aims and possible effects. The establishment of
the National Development Centre for School Management Training in
1983, several regional management consortia in 1989 and most recently the DES Task Force on Management Training in 1989, indicated the importance attributed to the work of headteachers and
senior staff in schools.

The development programmes increasingly promoted the idea of
the reflective practitioner, and drew on the work of such writers on
industrial management as Argyris and Schon (1974), Handy (1976,
1984), Adair (1983, 1985, 1986), Belbin (1981), Kolb *et al.* (1984) and
Hersey and Blanchard (1977). Management development programmes, however, have gradually lessened their earlier dependence
on models and theories derived from industry and commerce and have
increasingly drawn upon the values generated in the self-evaluation
and school improvement movements referred to earlier. Pehaps more
importantly, they have helped participants to articulate well grounded
responses to inappropriate proposals in which accountability is quan-
tified in terms of objective measures such as the number of GCSE or A
level passes, or other test results. Such simplistic measures run the

danger of reinforcing a view in which those features of schools which are most easily measured become the most important. There is a strong view within the profession that improvement is about enhancing the quality of learning experiences and valuing the less easily measured, but critically important *processes of education* rather than the products of schooling. The processes of education are not the same as industrial or commercial processes.

These perspectives – accountability, self-evaluation and school improvement, and management development – debated and contested in several different forums, have entered the education system alongside many other messages during a time of unprecedented change in which LEAs have been forced to make choices and to give priority to particular requirements at the expense of others. This has produced inconsistencies within the system and it is not surprising that even in 1991 some LEAs have not taken any major steps to prepare for the introduction of appraisal. It could hardly be otherwise given the rapidity with which systems of funding have been changed by central government. From 1986 onwards the three perspectives were to form a synthesis and become incorporated in principles of appraisal that have found a more accepting audience.

The ACAS report

The report on teacher appraisal undertaken by the Advisory, Conciliation and Arbitration Service (ACAS, 1986b) came about as a result of negotiations between the Government, the employers and the teachers' associations to try to settle a long-standing dispute about salaries, conditions of service and bargaining rights. An appraisal working party was set up and was required to report to the main committee. The report regarded appraisal as a positive process, designed to support and help teachers. It should aim to raise 'the quality of education by providing better job satisfaction, more appropriate in service training and better planned career development.' It also recommended the 'introduction of a well planned and well directed pilot project'. This led to the establishment of six DES funded, LEA pilot projects during 1987 and 1988. The report identified a set of principles that guided not only the pilot projects but also a range of additional appraisal initiatives undertaken by other LEAs. The report foresaw 'all teachers including headteachers being covered' and the nature and purpose of appraisal was to be understood:

> not as a series of perfunctory periodic events, but as a continuous and systematic process intended to help individual teachers with

their professional development and career planning, and to help ensure that the in-service training and deployment of teachers matches the complementary needs of individual teachers and the schools.

(ACAS, 1986b, para. 3)

While the report provided few details concerning the appraisal of headteachers, the references to individual development and the needs of schools made this fairly evident. By implication appraisal would help and inform headteachers as they engaged in processes relating to staff development. It would inform career development, give them feedback on performance and assist heads in making decisions relating to their schools.

ACAS (1986b, para. 5) saw the appraisal of headteachers as part of the responsibilities of the Chief Education Officer: 'who should appoint as appraiser an appropriate person with relevant experience as a Head Teacher, who will be required to consult with the designated Inspector responsible for the school and the designated Education Officer.' The Working Party also considered 'that, where necessary, each appraisal should benefit from a second informed opinion' (para. 5).

The National Steering Group report

The report of the National Steering Group on the School Teacher Appraisal Pilot Study is entitled *School Teacher Appraisal: a National Framework* and was published in October 1989 (NSG, 1989). It is based on data gathered from the six pilot LEAs (Croydon, Cumbria, Newcastle upon Tyne, Salford, Somerset and Suffolk), from pilot LEA coordinator conferences, from the evaluation of the pilot schemes undertaken by the Cambridge Institute of Education and from the National Development Centre, which acted as coordinating agency. The report places appraisal unequivocally within a developmental framework while acknowledging that teachers and headteachers do have responsibilities that should be effectively discharged.

Central government response

The NSG report identified the key principles and procedures which government regulations should prescribe under Section 49 of the Education (No. 2) Act 1986. It also indicated what should be contained in any related circular on the appraisal of teachers and headteachers. The Secretary of State, John MacGregor, responded in September 1990 and deferred the introduction of a national system, preferring to leave this decision to individual LEAs. On 11 December 1990, Mr Mac-Gregor's successor Kenneth Clarke stated his intention to introduce regulations requiring LEAs to arrange for half the teachers in service to have had a first appraisal by the end of the 1992–3 school year. In his letter to CEOs and the Interim Advisory Committee on Pay and Conditions of Service (IAC) he acknowledged that the recommendations of the NSG on the aims and methods of appraisal should, with some relatively small though possibly contentious modification, form the basis for the development of appraisal in the maintained sector. Circular 12/91 and the accompanying Regulations published in July 1991 were based on many of the NSG recommendations but there were significant additions. One such addition relates to salary and promotion. While there is to be no direct or automatic link between appraisal and promotion or additions to salary, 'it will be legitimate and desirable for headteachers to take into account information from appraisals, along with other relevant information, in advising governors on decisions about promotions and pay.' (Circular 12/91, para. 70). Other statements refer to school governors. The NSG made no reference to governor access to appraisal statements other than in terms of the resource implications which these might have. Under the Circular and Regulations copies of teachers' development targets are to be passed by the headteacher to chairs of governing bodies on request and in the case of headteachers copies of the complete appraisal statement (summary and targets) must be passed to chairs of governing bodies by the appraisers. Such additions and modifications are discussed in later chapters.

Summary

This chapter has outlined the background to headteacher appraisal. Three broad influences have influenced thinking on the features of appraisal: the accountability movement, the school improvement movement and an emergent management development perspective. The ACAS report of 1986 and the NSG report of 1989 provide the benchmarks against which the introduction of appraisal might be compared. Circular 12/91 and the Regulations are broadly based on the NSG report together with a number of significant additions. The long awaited Circular and Regulations frame the main features of a national scheme but leave scope for diversity. The range of approaches adopted in a number of early initiatives are outlined in the next chapter.

2

Systems of headteacher appraisal

While the ACAS and NSG reports identified many of the features which should characterize the appraisal of teachers there is less consensus over the form it might take in relation to headteachers. A number of models were adopted in the course of the six LEA pilot projects and more have emerged from work in other LEAs. Further formats have been proposed by individuals and groups arguing for specific approaches.

The purpose of this chapter is to identify some of the special features of headteacher appraisal and to outline the range of the methods that have been explored. Much can be learned in the process but it is important to bear in mind that participants in the various schemes were volunteers during a period when there was resistance from teachers and professional associations because of the dispute over teachers' pay and conditions of service. Some approaches were regarded by those who used or evaluated them as productive and imaginative but many are probably not suitable for wider adoption owing to their high cost. Nevertheless, they have raised awareness of issues, problems and possibilities concerning headteacher appraisal and these will no doubt be considered by LEAs, which now have responsibility for introducing headteacher appraisal into maintained schools. Whatever schemes are devised by LEAs, they will have to demonstrate sufficient consistency to justify the claim that they form part of a national system capable of benefiting all types of primary schools irrespective of their size, location and special features. The sheer number of primary schools makes this particularly challenging.

Special features of headteacher appraisal

While headteacher appraisal shares many of the processes of teacher appraisal there are features that are quite distinctive. The main features are set out below.

1 *Line management*   The 'line manager' of a headteacher is difficult to identify, unlike that of assistant teachers. There appears to be no one person who fulfils this role. LEAs have a strong management interest and may be required to exercise the authority invested in them should they feel that the school is being mismanaged in some way, but the actual line management link is not clear. Governing bodies have been given wide powers under the legislation enacted during the 1980s but the chair of governors can hardly be described as the head's line manager. There are other groups which have a legitimate interest in a school and the way it is managed and members of these may feel that the head has responsibility to them. Parents and members of the local community are an obvious example but again there is no line management connection. In general, governors, LEA officers and adviser/inspectors may request particular kinds of information which must be furnished by a headteacher and they may all hold views on the performance of a headteacher but they are not line managers in the accepted sense of the term. This situation makes the issue of who acts as a headteacher's appraiser particularly important.

2 *Role complexity*   The complexity of the primary headteacher's role and the widening range of tasks to be managed makes it impossible to appraise the whole of a head's job within a single appraisal cycle. The questions of who is to identify the specific aspects and how these are to be explored are central and sensitive areas of concern. While some teachers in primary schools carry management responsibilities these are unlikely to have the diversity associated with headship. In small schools, primary headteachers may also have responsibility for teaching pupils, which adds to the complexity of their role.

3 *Managing others*   Headteachers, to a greater degree than other members of staff, have to achieve goals with, and through, other adults. The appraisal of headteachers will therefore be as much concerned with the head's capacity to promote the professional development of staff, as with how he or she brings about improvements in the quality of learning that is offered to pupils in the school.

4 *A broad role set*   The role set of primary headteachers is likely to be wider than that of teachers, most of whom have full-time

responsibility for a class and are accountable to the head. Hence the process of information gathering will involve more respondents than is the case with teachers.

5 *The need for feedback*   Headship, even granting collegial forms of management, is a lonelier and more exposed role than that of teachers, who enjoy daily contact with their peers. These factors heighten the latent value of appraisal in the case of those headteachers who seek and value feedback on their performance. It is notoriously difficult for primary headteachers to gain 'accurate' feedback on their leadership, management styles and organizational behaviour because of their status and position in the school. Age differences between head and staff may also contribute to the problem.

6 *General lack of training for headship*   The appraisal of teachers takes place in the knowledge that they have received professional training in their core task – that of teaching. The majority of headteachers have received little systematic training in the management of schools, although more attention has been given to this in recent years. Any appraisal system for headteachers needs to be sensitive to the range of developmental needs likely to be expressed during the appraisal process.

7 *Follow-up support*   Support during the later stages of the appraisal cycle is important if the process is to be effective. Such support is likely to be less continuous for headteachers than for teachers, who are more likely to have the benefit of daily contact with their appraiser, usually the head or a deputy.

Given the factors outlined above, especially with regard to line management, it is important that headteacher appraisal is carried out by those who have experience of headship and are credible in the eyes of the appraisee. This almost certainly points to appraisers who are external to the school and this means that particular care must be given to establishing trust and confidence in the people involved in the system created.

Appraisal calls into play the interrelated processes of *disclosure* and *feedback*. The former is dependent on the appraisee's willingness to divulge information, thoughts and feelings which may be brought into play during the appraisal process. This requires a high level of maturity and self-confidence from the appraisee, and from the appraiser a capacity to observe events effectively, gather information with sensitivity, contextualize and interpret data and give feedback in ways that are acceptable to the appraisee. It also requires of the appraisee the ability and willingness to listen actively to feedback without premature closure or regression to defensive explanation.

The main challenge is to construct an appraisal system for primary headteachers that is appropriately rigorous, supportive and developmental and in which they actively seek feedback on their management skills. It should provide them with information on how effectively they have undertaken their stewardship of the school, and developed appropriate structures and processes for ensuring the quality of pupil learning and the enhancement of the work settings of all those employed in the school.

These, then, are the main features which differentiate headteacher from teacher appraisal. The pilot projects provide useful information on many of these issues and it is to these that we now turn.

Pilot schemes

All of the LEA pilot projects devoted most of their efforts to the appraisal of teachers but each gave some attention to headteachers, either during the lifetime of the projects (1987–8) or in extensions of such work supported by continuation funding. The following summaries, in alphabetical order, are based upon information contained in the NSG report (NSG, 1989) and in documents produced by the LEAs concerned.

Croydon

During the pre-project stage headteacher appraisal was linked to accountability as indicated in the following statement:

> The performance of headteachers in primary and secondary schools will be appraised by members of the inspectorate . . . In principle, the junior partners in these encounters will be appraised by the person normally considered to monitor and assist them in carrying out a major part of their work.
>
> (Croydon LEA, 1985)

As the pilot progressed this view changed and appraisal was presented more within a developmental and supportive framework. Over 90 per cent of all primary heads attended awareness raising sessions. About a quarter of these volunteered to attend a three-day planning and training workshop and from this a number of experiments were set up, including: two primary heads acting as appraisers to another head; a head and an LEA head/trainer working together as appraisers; a primary head and inspector working in consort; and a pair of heads appraising each other. The most successful appraisals involved *two* appraisers and the value of having a second appraiser, someone with a broad experience and knowledge of the LEA and its schools, was acknowledged.

Cumbria

A particular feature of the Cumbria scheme was a commitment to the view that headteacher and teacher appraisal should be preceded by a participative, collaborative whole school review. This review was seen as preparing for and supporting the introduction of appraisal into a school, while the outcomes provided a context within which appraisal could take place. Another headteacher and an adviser from the authority were involved as appraisers.

Headteachers selected their appraisers from a panel of trained heads. Each of the participants – appraisee, appraiser and adviser – selected an area of the head's work as a focus following initial discussions between the three parties. Three days were allocated to appraisal conferences (interviews), one day for each of the selected areas of headship. Each appraiser spent a day in the school observing the headteacher as she or he undertook various tasks and also collected information from relevant people. Given the proximity and potential overlap between school review and appraisal it is important to have a clear distinction between processes relating to school review and those relating to appraisal. We return to this matter in Chapter 3.

Newcastle upon Tyne

The Newcastle project was committed to the view that appraisal should be responsive to the individual context of the school. Appraisal teams/working groups were established in each pilot school. Whole school review was not regarded as a prerequisite to appraisal. The appraisal of headteachers was undertaken by a practising headteacher. Some cross-phase headteacher appraisals were also conducted. The LEA advisers attached to appraisees' schools were involved as consultants and the outcomes of the 'professional interview' were discussed with them and a senior LEA officer. A self-appraisal pro forma formed the basis of the main agenda for all appraisal discussions. It is reported that by allowing schools to produce their own schemes, within their LEA's formative framework, a high degree of ownership and commitment was generated.

Salford

The starting point was seen as the construction of 'an acceptable description of what the head is expected to do. It must cover areas deemed important by the employer and must be flexible enough to reflect the priorities dictated by the headteacher and by the school context.'

A generic job description was then drawn up by the headteacher and the governing body, following which key aspects were identified in negotiations between the headteacher and an appraiser. Some of these were selected for consideration, and others were retained for reference in future appraisals. The agreed aspects then formed the basis of self-appraisal, evaluation and discussion. During the initial stages of the process, relevant contextual factors were discussed and decisions made on what kind of information should be collected and who might collect it.

Four models of headteacher appraisal were piloted:

1 A 'validated partnership' model (peer appraisal moderated by a member of the project team).
2 A model involving two appraisers – a member of the project team and a practising headteacher.
3 A model involving two appraisers – a member of the project team and a general adviser.
4 A model using one appraiser, either a member of the project team or an adviser with experience as a headteacher.

Somerset

Somerset adopted the term 'review and development' in exploring appraisal. Each 'resident head' (appraisee) was appraised by two practising headteachers – a 'key reviewer' and a 'support reviewer' – from a similar phase but different catchment area. An LEA officer or adviser provided contextual information on the school, processed the agreed statement and monitored the outcomes for the resident headteacher. The review discussion was seen as a three-way process in which issues were identified, explored and resolved. Chairing and note-taking alternated between the two reviewers. Targets and action plans were agreed, and a final statement was signed by the three participants and countersigned by the CEO. A copy was placed on the appraisee's confidential file at County Hall.

Suffolk

Suffolk LEA had already carried out some experimental work two years before the pilot schemes were started. This was then linked to the national initiative when Suffolk became one of the pilot authorities.

The team gave much attention to the question of who should undertake the role of appraiser. Having considered alternatives, such as a

permanent team of seconded heads, heads on short-term release, practising headteachers and triads of heads who each appraised the others,
they concluded that 'the appraisal of headteachers is a complex process best tackled by a team approach.' Familiarity with the school and
LEA practices was regarded as essential. The appraisal would be undertaken by a team of three: a headteacher, the area officer or deputy,
and the school's link adviser. Initially emphasis was placed on the
development of the previously unknown role of consultant head but in
the national pilot particular attention was paid to clarifying the nature
of the joint responsibility of the team and the role of each member.

All undertook a four-day skills-based course. The three then met to
plan the appraisal and agree areas of focus and methods of data collection. The consultant head accepted main responsibility for collecting
and collating data and carrying out the dialogue. Seven days of supply
cover was allocated to the consultant head, two and a half days to the
appraisee or three where he or she was a teaching head. The consultant heads were expected to support the appraisees as they undertook
their action plan to achieve defined targets.

A classification of approaches

All the approaches for headteacher appraisal adopted in the pilot
projects involved practising heads in the role of appraiser and in most
cases they played the major part in the process. Experience of headship and the ability to contextualize information acquired at the information gathering stage and during the interview itself were regarded
as crucial. Each of the projects acknowledged the necessity to select
areas for specific focus and the need for these to be identified and
agreed by all the parties concerned.

Other schemes and suggestions for headteacher appraisal are to be
found outside the work of the pilot projects and these add further to
possible ideas which need to be considered in creating a generally
acceptable model. These, together with the approaches adopted in the
pilot LEAs, are now brought together to provide a classification of
headteacher appraisal possibilities. An analysis of published sources
relating to headteacher appraisal suggests seven approaches, here
called superintendent, task force, peer head(s) plus officer/adviser,
panel, peer, subordinate and evaluator. These are dealt with in turn.

The superintendent model

This model was proposed by Trethowan (1987). In his view, 'none of
the more recently proposed solutions to the problems of headteacher

appraisal meets the requirement of "feedback with responsibility".' By this he meant the need to have appraisers who owned the responsibility for following up an appraisal and providing appropriate support. The recommendation was that CEOs appoint an agent 'to manage the performance of headteachers and to conduct their appraisal and target setting sessions.' Such a role is similar to that of school superintendents in the United States, and could form a line management link between CEOs and schools. Within this model headteachers would be given detailed job descriptions and

> be answerable to a clearly indicated manager using undisputed criteria for assessment and accepted performance standards supported by annual reviews. Any head who failed, at this annual review, to achieve the agreed performance standards should be asked to account for the failure and the fault for lack of achievement should be clearly and fairly stated.
>
> (Trethowan, 1987, p. 164)

Five principal accountabilities of headteachers were identified: ethos and aims; planning and control; review and improvement of performance; appointment and development of staff; communication and relationships. The superintendent approach is responsive to some of the special features of headteacher appraisal but accountability assumes that sets of criteria and forms of assessment already exist and are uncontested, claims which are generally not supported by research.

Task force model

This approach was proposed by the Committee of Heads of Educational Institutions, comprising representatives of headteacher associations and principals of colleges. The committee proposed the creation of an independent task force of experienced heads who would be seconded to it for periods of from one to three years. Such a task force would be responsible to the senior chief inspector. The process would involve the professional appraiser, chair of governors and an elected member of the school's staff. Such a national system would undertake an appraisal 'in a period of up to three days', producing a confidential report to the appraisee head and the CEO. The Task Force would not be involved in follow-up support since it was assumed that this 'would continue by existing means'.

Gane (1986), in commenting on this proposal, calculated that 139 headteachers would be required for such a system, a figure equivalent to almost one-third of HMI. Such a model would not resolve the problem of contextual knowledge at LEA or school levels and would meet few of the special features required in headteacher appraisal.

Peer head(s) plus officer and adviser

Northamptonshire LEA produced a consultative document cited in Gane (1986) which expressed the value of a team approach in these words:

> Team appraisal is seen as being undertaken by a group of persons who share the dialogue according to an agreement about which area of accountability each member of the team individually shall cover. The benefit of the team approach is that a head is offered a variety of insights into his performance from colleagues, each having a different viewpoint.
>
> (p. 40)

While there are differences in the specific roles advisers and officers might take in this approach, the major process role is often allocated to the peer head(s) involved. The approach has the advantage of using those who should have credibility with their colleagues and it takes advantage of the contextual knowledge held by heads and advisers or officers. The viability of the model is, however, dependent on the existence of sufficient advisers and officers within an LEA. One of the benefits is that an LEA representative may facilitate resources necessary during the follow-up stage, thus meeting one feature of headteacher appraisal identified earlier. A further advantage is that it enables the LEA to monitor consistency within the overall system constructed for the appraisal of headteachers.

Panel appraisal

This approach has a wider team membership and has been reported on by a number of individual schools that have implemented schemes similar to that reported by Butler (1987). In Butler's account the deputy head, elected members of staff, teacher-governors, a governor, a member of the parent–teacher association, a senior adviser, a local headteacher and a member of the local business community formed the panel. The questions to be asked of the head were agreed and then given to the head and also published in the staff room. At the appraisal interview the panel engaged in discussions based on the head's written response to a ten-page questionnaire.

The terms of reference for the panel were as follows:

1 To appraise the head in terms of:
   (a) education (aims, objectives, curriculum, pastoral systems etc.);
   (b) management (organization, administration, communication, planning, resources, monitoring etc.);
   (c) internal relations (motivation and leadership of staff, staff development, pupils, discipline, control etc.);
   (d) external relations (parents, governors, community, LEA etc.).
2 To give recognition and praise to the headteacher for good performance.
3 To identify areas for improvement and development in the head's performance.
4 To identify areas for improvement and development within the school.

This is a large agenda to cover and it is difficult to see how such a wide range could be explored in depth during a single interview. Its strengths lie in the contextual knowledge brought by panel members together with the external perspective provided by others. The number of people involved, however, is likely to make organization of the process difficult and cumbersome.

Peer appraisal

Appraisal by other headteachers has been explored by groups of headteachers in a number of LEAs. Mountford (1988) has documented one such scheme in North Staffordshire. The headteachers operated in groups of five – four appraisers and one appraisee head who was also an appraiser in relation to one of the other four. All the heads had participated in an evaluation course before the scheme. Planning meetings by the appraiser quartet were held in participant schools. The deputy head of the appraisee's school collected the views of staff on the head's management systems using a list of prepared questions. The appraisers had access to a range of documents concerning the school and its organization. At the appraisal interview one of the appraiser heads acted as principal interviewer, asking prepared questions in relation to such aspects as external liaison and internal communication. The organization of teaching and learning within the school and pupil assessment were also included. Following the interview with the appraisee, the peer headteachers then interviewed the deputy head, who drew upon data he or she had collected during interviews with staff. An evaluation report was written and agreed at a subsequent meeting.

It was reported that each of the heads concerned respected the views of the others and all found the experience productive. The fact that each had participated in an evaluation course before constructing the scheme indicated the importance of training for all concerned.

This approach does provide an external perspective and involves the collection of data by an outsider. There is no reason why data collection of this sort should be restricted to the deputy head and other schemes have drawn on heads of year, curriculum coordinators and other 'middle managers'. The model did not, however, include obervation of the headteacher at work.

Subordinate model

Pyne (1987), a primary headteacher, integrated her own appraisal and that of staff by means of a series of confidential interviews. Within each interview staff were invited to comment on the management and organization of the school, how it had helped or hindered development, and to give their views on what was expected of the head and how she might improve on her performance. Willingness to disclose and the capacity to receive feedback were central features of the scheme. The increase in mutual trust, improved interpersonal relationships and a heightened sense of shared objectives were all cited as benefits of the approach.

It might be argued that such a scheme lacks an external perspective and would not be effective in situations where the headteacher was less open and willing to discuss sensitive matters in an unthreatening way. But it does have features compatible with the participative style of some primary schools and costs would not be high. However, it is not clear how the development of the head would be supported after such an appraisal, or to what extent and in what manner external support and resources might be mobilized.

The evaluator model

All the models referred to so far have been premised on the view that only those with experience of headship should be involved in the appraisal of headteachers, an assumption challenged by Turner and Clift (1988). They argue that any person skilled in the art of evaluation could be an effective appraiser. In their view, 'the key issue in a headteacher appraisal is that of adopting an appropriate methodology.' The most successful appraisals on which they reported were those in which appraisers effectively facilitated *self-evaluation*. For Turner and Clift the key was *the process*: 'a self evaluation can be facilitated by almost anyone who can provoke thought and self-criticism.' They concluded 'that a person without experience of headship is a potentially valuable person to conduct the appraisal of

Headteachers, but that such an appraisal needs to be based on more than an appraisal interview.' Task observation, staff interviews and use of documentary evidence should be included.

It is understandable that experienced evaluators such as Turner and Clift should come to this conclusion. Similar arguments have in the past been put forward in connection with the role that an external evaluator might play in the evaluation of the curriculum or of schools as organizations, and in countless projects of diverse kinds. But the rationale does not fit the prevailing logic of action and experience and is therefore likely, for the present at least, to be regarded as too radical.

Circular 12/91 and the Regulations state that headteachers will have two appraisers, both external to the school, one of whom must be either a practising headteacher, or who has been a headteacher in the appropriate phase and had experience relevant to current conditions in the appraisee's school. In the case of nursery schools the appraiser should, wherever possible, have experience of early childhood education. This provides appraisal bodies with some choices. They might draw upon a panel or task force of seconded heads, of recently retired heads, or use peer appraisers or some combination of both. Where LEAs have only a small number of secondary schools, some of them, aware of the competitive culture beginning to emerge in the secondary sector, are beginning to explore a reciprocal approach in which secondary heads from one LEA act as appraisees to their peers in the other. Headteachers, if for no other reason than their length of service, will differ in terms of their knowledge and maturity in the job. Some will be confident and seek inventive interpretations which aid the kind of appraisal they seek to undergo. There is nothing within the Circular to prevent a headteacher from drawing upon such forms as panel appraisal or subordinate appraisal referred to earlier, if they so wish. What is essential, and noted by the authors in their work with headteachers is the importance of having an adequate model of headteacher appraisal which kept conceptually distinct the processes of headteacher appraisal and school review. Appraisal might draw upon information derived from school review but its essential purpose is to constructively explore what the headteacher has done in seeking to effectively manage and lead the school and its endeavours. This aspect is explored in Chapter 3.

Summary

In this chapter the ways in which headteacher appraisal differs from that of assistant teachers were considered. The differences included:

problems in defining a head's line manager; the complexity of the role; emphasis on managing other adults; a broad role set; difficulty in obtaining feedback on performance; limited training; and the problems of obtaining support after the appraisal interview. The various approaches which might overcome some or all of these problems were then explored by reference first to the six appraisal pilot LEAs and then to other formats proposed by a range of individuals and groups.

These were categorized and discussed under the headings: superintendent, task force, peer head(s) plus officer/adviser, panel, peer, subordinate and evaluator models. The collection of information stage gives the appraisee plenty of scope and this, in turn, can radically shape the appraisal process. Circular 12/91 endorses this view. The appraisee is the locus of the process and can, through consultation, draw upon many features of the pilot schemes and models outlined here. The next chapter looks in more detail at issues relating to headteacher appraisal which must be addressed when attempting to operationalize Circular 12/91 and the associated Regulations.

_____ 3

_____ *A model for headteacher appraisal*

In Chapter 2 we examined various ways in which headteacher appraisal might be approached and we considered the nature of several pilot schemes and experiments set up by LEAs or schools in the 1980s. All of these were faced by a number of similar, *a priori*, questions which had to be answered in order to plan and implement their schemes. These were:

- What are the purposes of appraisal?
- Who should do the appraising?
- What should be appraised?
- What kind of contact should there be between appraisers and appraised?
- What information should be collected?
- What written record should be kept of the appraisal?

There has been, since the publication of the National Steering Group's report (NSG, 1989) and government responses to it in 1989, 1990 and 1991, a growing consensus on how these questions should be answered; although there are still differences of opinion about a few specific matters, as will be seen later.

In this chapter we discuss the questions above in the light of our own experience with several LEAs and indicate how practical solutions implemented by these authorities can lead to a generally acceptable model of headteacher appraisal that will fit within the guidelines embodied in Circular 12/91 and accompanying Regulations. The proposed model is later explained, justified and extended in Chapters 4, 5 and 6.

The purposes of appraisal

The aims and purposes of *teacher* appraisal are well documented in various reports (Suffolk LEA, 1985; ACAS, 1986b; NSG, 1989; DES, 1990a) but there is very little discussion regarding the specific purposes of headteacher appraisal in these or most other reports or documents on the subject. One reason for this is perhaps that most commentators regard appraisal as essentially a developmental process, whether applied to teachers or to headteachers, and there is, therefore, no need to distinguish between the two. The prime purpose of headteacher appraisal is to assist in raising professional standards, ultimately for the benefit of pupils.

The emphasis on development does not mean that accountability should have no significance at all in the appraisal process. It is unfortunate that, as indicated in Chapter 1, an apparently 'hard edged' approach underpinned many of the early discussions and proposals. This caused concern and opposition from teachers, headteachers and their professional associations. But few would dispute that a head is accountable to an employer (as is any employee) for carrying out work according to an agreed contract. In most organizations this 'contractual' accountability is implemented through a clearly defined line management system. But the identification of a line manager for a headteacher remains a difficult problem, especially since it falls between the competing demands of the chief officer, inspectors, advisers and chair of governors: a matter referred to in Chapter 2.

For this reason, the idea of contractual accountability associated with a line management system has been strongly resisted by heads. But the notion of *professional,* as distinct from *contractual,* accountability is seldom disputed. To be accountable as a professional is to work according to agreed standards and an accepted code of practice *vis-à-vis* clients and colleagues. The head is thus accountable for what he or she does that affects pupils and staff within the school. Discussion regarding the head's managerial role can scarcely be conducted without reference to such professional accountability and this must represent an important purpose of appraisal alongside its key developmental function.

But contractual accountability in terms of linking appraisal to pay, promotion and discipline remains a sensitive issue. Disclaimers such as 'There will be no automatic link between appraisal of performance or pay' (DES, 1991a) and, 'appraisal shall not form part of any disciplinary or dismissal procedures' (DES, 1991), are qualified by regulation 14 – (1) which states:

> Relevant information from appraisal records may be taken into account by headteachers, Chief Education Officers or any officers or advisers specifically designated by a Chief Education Officer . . . in advising those responsible for taking decisions on the promotion, dismissal or discipline of school teachers or on the use of any discretion in relation to pay.
>
> (DES, 1991)

The various statements together suggest that appraisal is not to be regarded primarily as a disciplinary or promotional tool but that if information is obtained as a result which has a bearing on these other processes it might be used accordingly. Some might argue that this is simply bowing to the inevitable and that it would be virtually impossible to isolate such information. It remains, however, a matter for future research as to whether and to what extent the inclusion of the above statement in the Regulations will adversely affect the implementation of positive and successful appraisals.

Given the uncertainties and anxieties which surround the purposes of headteacher appraisal, it is important that those managing or taking part in embryo schemes should be aware of these and come to some agreement regarding which are the most important purposes and how they might be accommodated within an LEA scheme. This matter is considered again in Chapters 4 and 7 where it is argued that raising awareness and building consensus about the purposes of appraisal is best done during initial training programmes.

It is possible to sum up the debate on the purposes of appraisal by suggesting that it is regarded as principally developmental but that it must inevitably deal with matters of accountability, especially professional accountability. There are several potential aims that might contribute towards achieving effective appraisal and it is important to discuss these with those who are involved with any proposed scheme, in order to reach a common understanding.

For the present, and pending further discussion in later chapters, it is suggested that development and accountability might be combined in the following statement.

> The main purpose of appraisal should be to improve the functioning of the school as it affects the services provided for its pupils and staff. Stemming from this the key objectives should be:
> ● to provide the opportunity for an outsider(s) to offer feedback, support and encouragement, and to assist the head to explore

his or her vision for the school, reviewing relevant aims, plans
and policies;
- to identify ways of improving the management of the school;
- to consider the head's professional development;
- to identify and discuss, frankly and openly, concerns about the
school, from whatever source they come.

The next question faced by those who plan and implement appraisal
schemes is: who should appraise a headteacher?

Who should appraise?

The guidelines produced by the NSG (1989) acknowledged that 'the
role of the headteacher is unique and complex' and recommended that
regulations issued by the Government should specify:

> that two appraisers should be appointed . . . one person with ex-
> perience as a head relevant to the current conditions in the phase
> in which the appraisee head works. The circular should indicate
> that when one appraiser is expected to play a larger role in the
> appraisal than the other, that role should be exercised by a person
> with this experience. It should also indicate that one of the ap-
> praisers should be a professional officer of the LEA.
>
> (NSG, 1989, p. 7)

This recommendation has, through Circular 12/91 and Regulations,
now been endorsed by the Government (DES, 1991).

The importance of headship experience

Appraisees will generally have more confidence in, and give more
credance to, an appraiser who has had experience as a headteacher,
especially if such experience has recently been gained in the same
phase as the appraisee head.

During the initial stage in the appraisal process, practising heads will
normally have the capacity to help their appraiser to identify areas of
work upon which to focus. As the appraisal proceeds they will be able
to stimulate thought and discussion on problems, raised by the appraisee, with which they are familiar. It is not expected that they will
provide answers to problems that arise, but they will have the kind of
understanding, generated by their own experience, that will enable
them to empathize and work alongside their appraisee in a common
learning situation. Such common learning provides an additional
bonus for those involved since appraiser heads can also be regarded as
participants in a joint developmental process (see Chapter 8 for

comments upon this point by an appraisee head). There is every likelihood that they will take something of benefit back to their own school
as a result of the appraisal.

The choice of a practising head as an appraiser raises two sensitive
questions. How should allocation of appraiser to appraisee be carried
out? Should it be possible for an appraisee to refuse to have the
allocated appraiser? A strong view has emerged from the pilot authorities that a headteacher should not be permitted to choose the appraiser. This view is endorsed by the Secretary of State in Regulation 8
– (1) which states 'The local education authority shall appoint two
appraisers for the head teacher of each controlled, county or special
agreement school maintained by them, after consulting the governing
body of the school' (DES, 1991).

In practice, to avoid possible problems which could arise over the
perceived credibility of the appraiser or past relationships that might
stand in the way, some LEAs have introduced a negative option
whereby the appraisee has the right to reject (normally only once) a
nominated appraiser. In such cases a second appraiser would be identified and allocated by the LEA from a pool or panel of appraisers.

LEA representation

Normally the LEA representative will be an inspector or adviser since
these are the people most likely to know the school and its background
but, in practice so far, their involvement has varied quite widely.

Unlike those in the secondary sector, most primary advisers have
themselves been headteachers – a factor that increases their credibility. Hellawell (1990) explored the perceptions held by primary
headteachers in two LEAs about LEA advisers and inspectors as
appraisers. Most felt that currently there was insufficient support for
them and their schools and that there was an increasing shift towards
an inspectorial role which would not fit well with the head's view of
what appraisal should be about. Furthermore, neither inspectors nor
advisers were regarded by the heads as their line managers and most
took the view that if LEA representatives were to be involved in
appraisal, their part should be limited to that of a lesser contributor
alongside others.

Most respondents had not been appraised at the time of Hellawell's
research and it is interesting to note that their later responses, after
they had been appraised, were more positive *vis-à-vis* the role of inspectors and advisers. Our recent work with a substantial number of
headteachers confirms that this shift of view can take place. The heads
concerned expressed considerable reservations at first about the

involvement of advisers in the proposed LEA scheme. As in Hellawell's sample, many saw the growing inspectorial function of the advisers as incompatible with a developmental model of appraisal. But, again, following completion of a pilot scheme, all of those involved changed their views and fully supported the inclusion of an adviser in the process (see also Chapter 8).

It seems that most benefit accrues where the adviser or inspector is able to:

- draw upon his or her broad contextual knowledge of the LEA and its systems;
- establish links to forms of support and resources outside the school;
- act as a general facilitator and moderator in terms of bringing consistency in style and format of appraisals across the LEA.

It has also been suggested by heads that the very presence of an LEA representative acting alongside an experienced head brings to the process a safeguard against charges of the appraisal being too 'soft centred' or 'cosy'.

Whether other officers, apart from inspectors or advisers, should take part in the appraisal is, as yet, an impossible question to answer. There have been some small experiments involving personnel officers and other staff from County Hall but this model has generally not been pursued. There is the problem of credibility – how well do such people know the schools and the complexity of a head's job? Furthermore, most are already committed to other kinds of work and time to fit in visits would be a major problem. For the present at least, therefore, it seems that the LEA representative role will be undertaken by an inspector or adviser and as our experience has been with LEAs that have used advisers we will, from now on, refer to the second appraiser as 'adviser'. Bearing in mind the time commitment necessary for advisers to be involved in several appraisals, we will assume that they will wish to play only a secondary role. They will normally take part in the initial meeting and appraisal interview but not be involved in the collection of information.

The role of governors

Few schemes have actually used governors directly as appraisers. While they are now far more involved in the affairs of primary schools than was the case before the 1986 Education (No. 2) Act and the 1988 Education Reform Act, there is still wide variation in the ways in which such involvement is exercised. Several commentators (Dean, 1986; Gane, 1986; Trethowan, 1987) have expressed reservations about the suitability of governors as appraisers. These reservations are echoed by most heads, who also see the involvement of governors as a threat to their own professional management of the school.

More importantly, perhaps, neither the national guidelines nor government responses to them have proposed other than the indirect involvement of governors. They are generally regarded as potential contributors of information towards the appraisal and might be interviewed as part of the process.

Finally, according to Circular 12/91 and Regulations 'the appraisers shall send copies of the appraisal statement to the chairman of the governing body of the school.' This is a matter of concern to some heads and is discussed again in more detail in Chapter 6. In general, the issue of governor involvement in appraisal in the future is considered in Chapter 9.

What should be appraised?

The National Steering Group report (NSG, 1989, p. 15) makes the point that:

> there is greater benefit to be gained from the examination in depth of a few specific areas, provided that the selection is balanced and that key aspects of the head's work are not neglected over a long period. We therefore believe that the Circular should recommend arrangements which, in the majority of cases, specify areas of focus at the outset.

This, to most heads, makes good sense. The role is complex, involving many diverse responsibilities, and to attempt to deal with them all in the limited time available in any one appraisal cycle would be to do justice to none. Focusing down is therefore essential, but focusing on what?

There are two factors which should be considered. First, a fundamental concern of appraisal is with the way in which the head manages the school as distinct from the outcomes of such management. This relates to the difference between headteacher appraisal and school review. Second, it is necessary to select from the various areas of responsibility to which the head applies his or her management skills and experience. This is a matter of focus. The two factors are now considered in turn.

The difference between school review and headteacher appraisal

A school review will generally seek to obtain information on how effectively a school is performing, judged according to various *out-*

comes, such as the delivery of the curriculum, academic results, general behaviour patterns etc. The appraisal of the head, while not ignoring information obtained from a school review, will tend to concentrate more upon the *process* by which the head manages the school rather than the *outcomes* of that management. It is in their role as senior managers responsible for managing all that happens within the school, including, and especially, the work of their staff, that heads are appraised.

Questions that arise in connection with the process will be addressed to matters such as how the head initiates, supports, supervises and monitors policies for, say, curriculum development or budgetary control. Thus, for instance, a school review might indicate that, although a curriculum policy for science exists, evidence of its implementation in the school is hard to find. In the appraisal process it is the head's role as manager of the science coordinator, or even the manager of the deputy to whom the coordinator reports, which should be the focus of attention. To what extent has the head ensured that the policy is clear, has been communicated to all to whom it has relevance and is understood by them? This does not imply that the head should actually write the policy and personally supervise its implementation but rather that he or she should effectively manage the process by which it is achieved.

Areas of focus

There are many ways in which a head's role can be analysed and subdivided into categories of work or responsibility. These are considered in some detail in Chapter 4 but, for the present, we suggest that there are four broad areas of school management for which a head is responsible. We refer to them as the management and development of:

- teaching, learning and the curriculum;
- staff;
- finance and physical resources;
- external relations.

There is a fifth area which relates to them all and which we refer to as:

- the head's own 'professional development', which takes into account the acquisition and improvement of all those skills and competencies necessary to meet the increasing demands of the job as well as personal and career development.

Appraisal will therefore concentrate on agreed aspects of the four areas mentioned above plus the head's own professional development.

Contact between appraiser and appraisee

There is a tendency to associate appraisal mainly with the appraisal interview. This is usually the most visible manifestation of the process and the one which, at first sight, seems to offer the most tangible opportunities for positive (or negative) outcomes. A great deal of appraisal training is devoted to handling the interview and the very thought of the encounter often creates anxiety for appraisers and appraisees alike. It can be a long meeting (perhaps three hours or more) and requires intense concentration and sensitivity. It also has to accommodate the views of three people, each of whom may bring to bear a different perspective on the matter under review.

For the interview to be successful in terms of the agreed purposes there has to be adequate preparation and follow-up and these aspects of appraisal usually require much more contact between appraiser and appraisee than just the main interview. The following are important.

Preliminary contact   The first contact usually takes place before the parties have met in their formal roles. It is at this stage that the appraiser introduces herself or himself, explains the procedures to be adopted and agrees dates for subsequent meetings. The contact will usually be by telephone but may also involve correspondence and the exchange of documents.

Initial meeting   The appraisee and the main (headteacher) appraiser, accompanied by the second appraiser, will meet (usually at the appraisee's school) mainly to discuss and agree the focus of the appraisal and the collection of information, including any arrangements for observation. This is now regarded by most of those who have experienced appraisal as an essential first step and is a meeting that can take two hours or more (see Chapters 4 and 8).

Information gathering   During the information collection phase the appraiser and appraisee will normally meet for the second time. The head may meet the appraiser when introducing him or her to those who have agreed to be interviewed. There will also probably be further contact when the appraiser observes the head carrying out a task specified for observation. Finally, the two may want to share comments on progress at the end of the visit.

The main interview   This has already been mentioned and is regarded as the central part of the process which normally takes a substantial period of the time. It is dealt with in detail in Chapter 5.

Follow-up meetings   Sometimes the appraisal statement is written on the same day as the actual interview but some appraisers and appraisees prefer to let a little time elapse in order to digest the implications of the appraisal before starting the recording process. In the latter case they may arrange to meet again within a few days of the main interview in order to agree the wording of the appraisal statement and any targets associated with it.

Finally, there is a required follow-up meeting in the second year of the programme to review progress and to assist the appraisee to achieve targets, either by way of advice or other means (see Circular 12/91, paras 58 and 59). As the programme enters the second cycle it is likely, if the appraiser has not changed for any reason, that a new round of meetings between the same people will commence. There is therefore the opportunity for an ongoing dialogue between professional partners based upon a number of pre-arranged and carefully planned meetings.

Information for appraisal

The various key reports from ACAS, DES and NSG regarding teacher appraisal all stress the need for information to ensure cogent and productive discussion leading to appropriate developmental targets. There is a similar need for information in headteacher appraisal although, as some of the pilot projects have indicated, the sources may be different.

Sources of information for headteacher appraisal

There are four main sources of information that will assist in the appraisal of headteachers:

1 The appraisee's own knowledge.
2 Documents.
3 Observed situations.
4 Formal and informal interviews and questionnaires.

1   The head inevitably possesses a great deal of knowledge about the school and how it is managed that will be of use in his or her appraisal. In the pilot projects, attempts were generally made to tap this knowledge by encouraging the process of self-reflection. This was normally done through the use of a self-evaluation questionnaire, although sometimes the head agreed to keep a diary or log, or to write a statement about his or her vision for the school. Personal knowledge will also underpin the interview discussion where the appraiser will, for some of the time at least, encourage the head to reflect upon her or his role in managing the school.
2   There are various documents that may be helpful in appraisal. These include, for instance, school development plans, curriculum

policies, inspection reports, statistics relating to pupil numbers, test results etc. These can all be made available to the appraisers to help them to build up their understanding of the school and how it is managed.

3   An essential part of the appraisal of teachers is observation in the classroom. The same applies to heads who teach on a regular basis. But there are other tasks on which a head might be observed, such as chairing meetings, interviewing, monitoring the work of others and so on.

4   There are many people in, or associated with, the school who may be able to provide valuable information. The appraiser might therefore wish to interview some or all of the following: deputies, teachers, parents, governors, advisers who know the school well, other regular visitors to the school. Questionnaires may also be of help in collecting information from a wider group of people who, for whatever reason, cannot be interviewed.

Problems of collecting information

There is normally an abundance of information available but limited time in which to collect and analyse it. Some information may also be of a sensitive nature or difficult to obtain.

The appraiser and appraisee, therefore, have some important decisions to make. What information is needed? Are there priorities? How much time is available and how should it be used? Who should collect the information and how? Should there be any restrictions on the appraiser in asking questions? How confidential should be the information obtained? Should respondents remain anonymous as far as the appraisee is concerned? How much of the information should be recorded and what should happen to the notes?

These are some of the issues about which the appraiser(s) and appraisee should reach agreement, and a common understanding on such matters should form the basis of a 'contract' between the parties; a matter taken up again in Chapter 4.

Written records

'Appraisal statements' form the only written record of the appraisal process. It is recommended in the national guidelines that all other records be destroyed. The Government response to the guidelines (DES, 1990b, p. 7) states that: 'After each appraisal interview the appraisers, in consultation with the appraisee, shall prepare an appraisal statement recording the main points made in discussion and the conclusions reached, including targets.' How long and detailed such documents should be is a matter of preference and expediency but if the guidelines are interpreted literally, the recording of 'main points and conclusions' would not seem to demand a lengthy report; probably no more than a page.

Targets are a different matter and these will normally require more detail if they are to provide clear aims and direction for the appraisee. The elements of the appraisal statement, including targets, are dealt with in more detail in Chapter 6.

The ownership and use of the appraisal statement is a matter of some concern to heads. Regulation 13 – (2) provides that in the case of the headteacher:

> the appraisers shall provide a copy of the appraisal statement to the chairman of the governing body of the school and, in the case of the head teacher of a school maintained by a local education authority, to the Chief Education Officer or any officer of or adviser to the authority specifically designated by the Chief Education Officer;

Some heads are anxious that the document may contain information which is critical of them or could be interpreted as such and thus be detrimental to their careers. The right of the chair of governors to receive the appraisal statement involves that person much more in the appraisal process than many heads feel is justified. The sending of a copy of the statement to the CEO or person designated by him or her is also seen as threatening, not least because the document could potentially reach a wider audience than was intended.

This may well turn out to be an anxiety that has been over-emphasized. Statements (which have to be agreed by all parties) can almost certainly be written in a non-judgemental, non-critical way and still serve their purpose. Here, experience will probably prove to be a reassuring factor. This issue is discussed again in Chapter 6.

A model for headteacher appraisal

From the discussion of the issues above and our experience of working with several LEAs in planning, implementing and evaluating schemes, it is possible to construct a model for the appraisal of headteachers that will be acceptable within the proposed national guidelines and regulations and feasible in terms of resource requirements. The model contains the following elements.

1 The purpose of the appraisal will primarily be developmental, although always taking cognizance of professional accountability.

First year

Allocation of appraiser to appraisee.

Self-evaluation by appraisee including completion of pro forma.

Initial meeting between appraisers and appraisee. Negotiation and agreement of the appraisal contract including focus and information collection.

Observation by appraiser and collection of information as agreed in contract.

Appraisal interview involving appraisee, appraiser head and LEA adviser. Appraisal statement and targets agreed.

Second year

Implementation of action plans by appraisee to achieve targets.

Follow-up meeting between appraisee and appraiser to review progress towards targets and other pertinent matters that have arisen.

Figure 3.1   A two-year headteacher appraisal model.

2 The headteacher will be appraised by another headteacher with experience in the same phase, accompanied by an adviser; both appointed by the LEA.
3 The appraisal will concentrate upon the head's role as manager and a distinction will be drawn between whole school review and appraisal. During each two year cycle, the appraisal will focus upon two main areas of the head's role and upon the head's own professional development.
4 Contact between the appraisers and appraisee should include an initial meeting, the main interview and a follow-up meeting one year later.

5 Information for the appraisal should be collected on the basis of a carefully planned programme and the ground rules, roles and responsibilities for this should be incorporated in a 'contract' drawn up at the initial meeting.

6 The appraisal statement will be the only written record of the appraisal. It will contain a summary of the main points discussed, together with details of the targets agreed.

The structure of the model over two years can be illustrated in tabular form as in Figure 3.1.

A more detailed action plan adapted from one now in use by an LEA is set out in Appendix 5.

Summary

In this chapter the various issues arising from the national pilot projects and other schemes used in schools and LEAs were identified and examined. These included: the purposes of appraisal; who should appraise; what should be appraised; contacts between appraisers and appraisee; information for appraisal; written records of the appraisal.

A model for appraisal was then suggested and in Chapters 4, 5 and 6 we elaborate upon this. We suggest ways in which it might be implemented and possible solutions to problems that might arise.

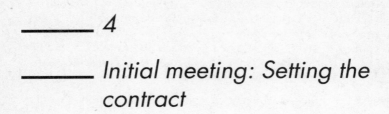

4

Initial meeting: Setting the contract

Following the selection and allocation of appraisers to appraisees by the LEA, the model for appraisal, as described in Chapter 3, continues by way of a number of carefully defined steps. The 'initial meeting' is a crucial part of this process and is considered in detail in this chapter, beginning with the roles of the three participants.

Roles in the appraisal process

In training workshops provided for one LEA the roles which each party in the appraisal process should play were discussed and eventually accepted by appraisers, appraisees and advisers. They reflect a consensus on the need for self-evaluation and on the collegial nature of the exercise. Development leading to school improvement was regarded as the essence of the process but professional accountability was introduced through the representation, by the appraiser head and adviser, of the interests and perspectives of key stakeholders in the process – especially pupils, staff, parents, governors and the LEA. Agreed roles for the three participants were as follows.

The appraisee's role
The appraisee's role will be that of a self-evaluating professional seeking information and feedback in order to achieve professional development leading directly, or indirectly, to school improvement.

The headteacher appraiser's role

The headteacher appraiser will act as an objective outsider or colleague bringing to the process the perspectives of all those with a relevant stake or interest in the school. He or she will act as manager of the process and will be responsible for: bringing the parties, including the adviser together; negotiating the appraisal contract referred to below; the conduct of the initial meeting and the main interview; ensuring that an agreed appraisal statement together with targets is produced; arranging and conducting any follow-up meetings.

The adviser's role

The adviser represents the local authority and will, through experience gathered in the appraisal process with other heads, seek to ensure consistency of procedures across the LEA. This should be helpful to participants in building supportive relationships extending beyond the boundaries of the individual school. The adviser should also be able to offer information, advice, support and, sometimes, resources that will help in the appraisal process and in attaining agreed targets.

Preliminary contact and preparation

The appraiser will, normally, first make contact with the appraisee by telephone in order to introduce herself or himself and to arrange a date for the initial meeting. Alternative dates will also be explored, even at this early stage, for the main interview so that the appraiser can make arrangements for the adviser to be present. The difficulty of finding dates for three busy people to meet for the main interview should not be underestimated and it may be that LEA advisory services will need to plan well ahead.

Next, the appraiser will normally write to the appraisee confirming the date for the initial meeting and send any documents which may be helpful to the appraisee in preparing for the meeting. The appraiser may also request details about the school that will save time when the parties meet. The appraiser will normally be supplied by the LEA with all the documents necessary for the process and will remain in control of these throughout the process. The letter from the appraiser to the appraisee confirming arrangements and giving further information might read as follows.

Dear —

Further to our telephone conversation I am writing to confirm our first meeting when we will discuss and agree the detailed procedures to be followed and the particular areas of headship that may form the focus of the appraisal. We will also need to decide upon the information that will be necessary to support our later discussions and how this can best be obtained.

To help you think about which areas might be covered in the appraisal I am enclosing a self-evaluation pro forma. The main part of this is for your own benefit and it will be for you to decide whether to give me a copy or not. There are, however, two pages at the back which I would like you to return to me before we meet. One asks the question:

'What is your vision for the school over the next few years?'

In other words, how would you really like the school to develop, despite the constraints which you will, no doubt, have to contend with along the way. Please write more on this if you so wish.

The final page asks you to suggest two areas of your work which you might like to concentrate upon during the appraisal. As you will see from the first question on the pro forma it is assumed that your role can be divided into four main areas, i.e. management and development of: (a) teaching, learning and the curriculum, (b) staff, (c) finance and physical resources and (d) external relations. Your response will be regarded purely as a suggestion at this stage since we will discuss the matter in some depth when we meet. We will also want to consider at the meeting how best to approach the separate, but related area of your own professional development.

Finally, I would appreciate any document(s) that will give me some background information about your role and about the school. If you have a job description it would be useful for me to see that. A prospectus or annual report to governors would also be helpful. The main purpose is to save time by answering some basic questions which I would otherwise have to ask when we meet.

I look forward to working with you soon.

Once the pro forma (a copy of this is included as Appendix 1) has been completed and the various documents returned to the appraiser the two parties are then prepared for the initial meeting.

The purposes of the initial meeting

The purposes of the initial meeting are set out in Circular 12/91, paragraph 45. They are:

to consider the head teacher's job description, in the context of the school's policies and development plan;

to agree the timetable and scope of the appraisal, identifying any areas of the appraisee's job on which the appraisal might focus;

to agree arrangements for any classroom observation;

to agree on the methods other than classroom observation by which information for the appraisal should be collected.

The National Steering Group report (NSG, 1989) on which the Circular is largely based emphasized that 'The clarification of sources and methods of collecting information for the appraisal should be a particularly important function of this meeting for heads, given the diversity of their work.' One other difference between teacher and headteacher appraisal is that classroom observation may not always be applicable for heads, in which case other forms of task observation may take its place.

Underlying all of the functional purposes of the initial meeting, as set out above, is an important psychological factor – the need to build *trust and confidence*. This can generally only be achieved through careful negotiation and joint decisions which form the basis of a *contract* between the two parties (see Circular 12/91, para. 49).

A contract is important for a number of reasons. There will normally be some apprehension and uncertainty surrounding the appraisal process and both parties may feel this. An appraisee head is allowing another person to examine in some detail certain aspects of his or her work and this can, understandably, create anxiety. But the appraiser may also feel anxious, perhaps for fear of exposing a lack of knowledge on some matters or of failing to exhibit due sensitivity. There is a risk that a wrong word or step could lose the respect or friendship of a valued colleague.

Although the notion of a contract in these circumstances may sound formal or legalistic there are good reasons for considering why and how it might be appropriate. The essence of a legal contract is an agreement based upon 'offer and acceptance' of certain promises by the parties concerned. If the actions associated with these promises are fully understood and agreed upon then the element of uncertainty can be considerably reduced.

Trust and confidence as far as the appraisee is concerned will come from: a sense of control over the process; the consultative aspects of negotiation; the committing to paper of what will happen, when and how; and the knowledge that agreed boundaries have been drawn around the actions that may take place. The test of the strength of the contract lies in the extent to which it reduces surprise, not so much in the outcome but in the process itself. Both parties should have a sense of knowing what will happen.

The elements of the initial meeting

In order to comply with the purposes of the initial meeting as set out on page 41 and to create an acceptable contract for all of the parties concerned there should be three key elements to the meeting. These are to:

- confirm common understanding regarding the purpose of the exercise;
- reach agreement on the focus of the appraisal;
- consider what information should be collected, how and by whom.

These are now dealt with in turn.

A common understanding regarding the purposes of appraisal

It is the intention here not to discuss again the aims and purposes of appraisal but rather to consider the question of how an appraiser and appraisee, meeting for the first time within the context of their temporary roles, might come to share a common view as to the aims and purposes of the joint task upon which they are about to embark. It is likely that unless there are clear guidelines to which both subscribe there will be differences of perception which could have a detrimental effect upon the process. So where should these guidelines come from and how should those who will use them be persuaded of their validity? Clearly, training for both appraisers and appraisees is important and it would seem sensible that, during training, the aims and purposes of appraisal should be regarded as a matter for continuing debate and refinement (see Chapter 7).

When the appraiser and appraisee meet to draw up their plans they should have shared a common experience in which a full and detailed discussion of aims and purposes has taken place. During their planning meeting, as an essential lead into the contract between them, they should reaffirm and write down those aims which they wish to adhere to. It is assumed that these will be in line with any written statement made by the LEA following consultation and training activities.

There may be many different approaches to appraisal – indeed John MacGregor, as Secretary of State, appeared to encourage diversity through his statement: 'I hope that LEAs will give as much freedom as possible to schools to develop detailed arrangements which suit their own particular needs and circumstances' (MacGregor, 1990). Circular

12/91 (para. 5) also refers to the opportunity for appraising bodies 'to give schools scope within the regulations to put in place arrangements for appraisal'. Different schools may therefore wish to emphasize some purposes of appraisal more than others although it is likely that the process will generally be regarded as developmental (see Chapter 3) and thereby will seek to improve the management of the school in order to improve the services it offers to its pupils and staff.

Once the purposes of the appraisal have been agreed the two parties will then concern themselves with the second issue – which parts of the headteacher's work to appraise.

The focus of appraisal

A headteacher has a complex role and is responsible to many different people for managing all aspects of school life. The potential for ambiguity and uncertainty are considerable. Planning and policy-making represent rational attempts to bring order to the complex flux of events as they occur within the school. But these procedures, in themselves, and the head's responsibility for them, add extra dimensions to an already extensive role.

The appraiser, in cooperation with the appraisee head, therefore faces a difficult task. Within the time available (usually no more than two days for the whole process) it would be impossible to appraise more than a small part of the head's overall job. The problems are:

1 how to reduce this complex and diverse set of tasks and responsibilities to a comprehensive but manageable set of categories;
2 how to choose from these categories certain areas that seem appropriate for a particular head and school at a particular time.

We will deal with (1) and (2) in turn.

Areas of responsibility

The evaluation report on the national schoolteacher appraisal pilot project (Cambridge Institute of Education, 1989) points to the fact that headteacher appraisal inevitably focuses attention on the head's role and leads to a closer scrutiny of contractual obligations. 'It is also clear that in a number of authorities, existing documentation is thin (possibly inadequate) and provides a poor starting point.' This is diplomatic language. The fact is that there is considerable confusion regarding the exact nature of a head's role and responsibilities and this is increasingly so as the overall management of schools and associated power structures shift, following the Education Reform Act and other government measures relating to terms and conditions of employment.

What the literature (including a variety of job descriptions by some LEAs) provides is a long and varied list of duties, tasks and behaviours which are considered necessary for effective headship. Examples of such lists can be found in Leithwood and Montgomery (1986), Trethowan (1987), Moore (1988) and Maiden and Harrold (1988). The longest of these lists contains thirty-four items ranging from responsibility for first aid and checking new equipment to making policy decisions.

What is needed is a way of classifying or categorizing a wide-ranging set of responsibilities and tasks into broad areas so that an appraiser and appraisee can agree to focus upon certain of these and, within them (for inevitably they will be broad), upon certain aspects considered to be important. We have discussed this issue in several training workshops and a model that reduces the number of areas to five has been tried and generally found acceptable to heads. Figure 4.1 shows a 'map' of the 'Areas' of headship. These are explained below, and followed by examples of 'Aspects' that might be focused upon within those areas. (From here on, throughout the book, capitals will be used for the first letters of 'Area' and 'Aspect' when the terms are used in the special sense explained below.)

Within the wheel in Figure 4.1 there are four Areas – the management and development of: teaching, learning and the curriculum; staff; finance and resources; and external relations. From discussions with heads and advisers these appear to be comprehensive and to embrace all of the responsibilities of the headteacher's role.

At the hub of the wheel there are 'policies, structures, monitoring and evaluation'. This implies that the school will have policies and organizational structures through which the policies can be implemented in all four Areas. It also indicates that such policies will be subject to critical review through periodic monitoring and.evaluation. The appraisal process is part of this review, albeit one specifically concerned with the head's role as manager of the four Areas. It will, therefore, be necessary for the appraiser and the head to select appropriate Areas: a point taken up again later.

In addition to the four Areas within the spokes of the wheel 'professional development' is shown as the rim – holding the wheel together, as it were. This implies that embracing and affecting all Areas of a head's responsibilities will be his or her own development. This will include knowledge, skills and attitudes and all other aspects of personal and career development that contribute to the growth of the head as a manager.

An appraiser and appraisee about to select one or more of the Areas will soon realize that each, in itself, is extensive and involves

Figure 4.1 Areas of headship.

many Aspects of work relating to it. It is therefore necessary for the parties to spend some of their time considering the particular Aspects which seem important. Two examples are set out below. These are not necessarily comprehensive and readers may wish to add to or amend the lists as appropriate and to construct their own lists for the other Areas.

One Area, 'The management and development of staff', might, for instance, include the following Aspects:

Interviewing and selection procedures
Induction of new staff
Role/job descriptions
Staffing structures
Decision-making procedures
Communication systems
Motivation and incentives

Discipline
Staff development policy
Identification of needs
Appraisal scheme

Another Area, 'professional development' might be sub-divided as follows:

General competencies
  problem-solving
  communication
  decision-making
  delegation
  interpersonal skills
  planning
  time management
Future plans
  priorities for coming year
  constraints affecting performance
  career progression/development
  training needs

It will be noted that the 'general competencies' referred to under 'professional development' are applicable to each of the four Areas set out in Figure 4.1. This indicates that the head's professional development is a key Area that should always be included in the appraisal process.

Each of the five Areas can thus be divided into sub-sections referred to as Aspects. An Aspect, in itself, can still represent a broad and complex set of tasks. For instance, within 'management and development of staff' the Aspect 'staff development policy' might include not only the plans and policies themselves but also how they were drawn up, how those responsible for them were selected and supported during the process and procedures for monitoring and updating them etc. It is, therefore, assumed within each Area only some of the many possible Aspects will be dealt with. Examples of Aspects in all the Areas referred to above are included in Appendix 2.

Selecting the Areas and Aspects

How many and which Areas should be selected for appraisal, and by whom? Circular 12/91 suggests that appraisal will be more 'purposeful' if it focuses upon specific areas of work (para. 20) and that the selection of areas of focus should be 'balanced' so that key aspects of work are not neglected over a long period (para. 46). The NSG, drawing on the experience of the pilot authorities, reports:

In three pilot LEAs heads and their appraisers have been required to select between them a small number of areas of focus – normally three – on which appraisal would concentrate. Where specific areas have been identified the collection of information has been tailored accordingly.

(NSG, 1989, p. 14)

This seems logical given the considerable diversity of tasks for which a headteacher is responsible and the limited time available to carry out the appraisal. Our own experience with several LEAs suggests that out of the four Areas referred to earlier two should be selected in each two-year cycle. It is assumed that in the next cycle the two other Areas will normally be chosen unless there are good reasons for not doing so. Furthermore, whatever the Areas chosen there should always be the opportunity to discuss the head's own professional development, making three Areas in all.

Selection of the Areas and Aspects within them will take place during the initial discussion and will normally be a matter for negotiation. In practice it seems appropriate that the appraisee should select those Areas which he or she feels are most relevant at that time. This means that there should be some prior reflection on this question; hence the use of the pro forma referred to earlier and discussed in more detail in Chapter 5. The appraiser's role in this could well be that of a sounding board, asking the question, 'why choose those particular Areas?' Negotiation then becomes a matter of the head justifying his or her choice.

Critics of this approach may suggest that it is too 'soft' and might allow the appraisee to avoid issues that should be confronted. Against this, it can be argued that in the initial stages of appraisal when there may, for many headteachers, be considerable uncertainty or anxiety surrounding the process, it is more important to build confidence by offering to them this element of control. Furthermore, it will be expected that in the next cycle other Areas will be dealt with and it will not be possible always to avoid difficult issues.

Obtaining information

In Chapter 5 the various kinds of information that might be useful in the appraisal process and the possible ways in which they might be collected are discussed in some detail. Here we consider how, given the time constraints and the need to build and maintain trust and confidence, arrangements for collecting information might be made and what kind of documentation might be useful to support the contract.

There are three key points to take into account in drawing up the part of the contract relating to the collection of information.

1 The collection of information can and should take place within the 'Guidance and code of practice' which is set out in Annex A attached to Circular 12/91 (see Chapter 5), and
2 Both parties should agree and fully understand their responsibilities with regard to the collection and subsequent use of the information.
3 Information will be collected only in those Areas and for those Aspects of the head's role already agreed.

An example will serve to illustrate how agreement relating to the collection of information will normally form the major part of the contract.

- Assume that one Area selected for appraisal is the 'management and development of staff' and that 'staff development policy' is regarded as a key Aspect. In discussion, the appraiser and appraisee consider the following to be important: the effectiveness of the staff development committee; the place of the staff development policy in school life; perceptions of staff about the current priorities and programme; views of staff regarding satisfaction of their own development needs.
- Arrangements are then made for the collection of information. It is suggested that, after reading policy documents, the appraiser should visit the school on a day coinciding with a meeting of the staff development committee. The head will arrange meetings with members of staff who have taken part in, or benefited from, staff development activities and others who have had little involvement. The appraiser will meet members of the staff development committee, observe the meeting and otherwise be free to talk to any member of staff during break time or the lunch period.
- Agreement is also reached to concentrate on specific questions, such as the views of all staff on the policy itself – especially whether they know of its existence, what it contains and whether they felt they had played a part in drawing it up.
- The staff development coordinator and members of the committee will arrange to talk briefly to all members of staff about 'personal needs in a time of rapid change' and report back to the head on this matter.
- A questionnaire, covering the views of staff on the value and outcomes of the past year's programme, will be drawn up, administered and analysed by the committee. A report on this will be made available to the head and appraiser.

A number of points can be made about the above example. First, it is set out in some detail to indicate as clearly as possible the understanding that might be reached by the appraiser and appraisee. In practice, it would be abbreviated and could, in note form, be incorporated under four columns headed 'Area and Aspects', 'Appraiser to', 'Appraisee to' and 'Comments' on a single side of A4 paper (see Appendix 4). Second, it is important to note that the responsibility for the collection of information is shared. Not only the appraiser but also the head, the staff development coordinator and members of the staff development committee are involved. Third, the spreading of the information load in this way enables the appraiser to focus on more than one Area of appraisal. In fact, interviews with staff, questionnaires, observations etc. could be used to ascertain information on more than one Area. Time can thus be used to best advantage, a point taken up again in Chapter 5.

Summary

The term contract is used to signify an agreement between the parties to the appraisal process which, in order to build up trust and confidence between them, is embodied in a short written statement. The agreement is mainly arrived at during a preliminary meeting between appraiser and appraisee that addresses certain key issues.

The first relates to a common understanding concerning the purpose or purposes of the appraisal, taking into account the particular needs of the head and of the school at a particular time. Agreement on this issue will be helped if those involved have previously discussed the nature and purpose of appraisal at a training workshop.

The second issue concerns the focus of the appraisal, given that it would be impossible to include all parts of a headteacher's role at once. Four major Areas of responsibility are suggested – the management and development of: teaching, learning and the curriculum; staff; finance and budgeting; and external relations. Two of these Areas should be dealt with in any one appraisal cycle. In addition, the Area of the head's own professional development should always be included. The Areas themselves are large and complex and in order to deal with them in reasonable depth they should be sub-divided into Aspects.

The third issue concerns the collection of information. What is needed? Who collects it and how? This matter requires careful negotiation and when agreed should be written down along with the purposes and the Areas and Aspects to form the appraisal contract. A short form which might be used for writing a contract is set out in Appendix 4.

_____ 5

_____ *Information for appraisal*

In Chapter 4 the initial meeting leading to an agreed contract between the parties to the appraisal process was discussed. An essential part of that contract relates to the collection of information deemed necessary for appraisal purposes and it was suggested that the nature of the information obtained and the manner in which it is obtained are crucial elements in the agreement. The contract must be based on common understanding if the necessary trust and confidence are to be built up from the start. In this chapter it is proposed to examine in more detail:

- the need for information;
- its nature and source;
- issues associated with its collection and use.

The need for information

The importance of information in promoting and underpinning discussion about the head's role in managing the school seems fairly obvious. How can an appraiser ask pertinent questions and help the head to come to clearly thought out conclusions unless the interviewer has knowledge of the issues under discussion?

The matter is not, however, as straightforward as it may seem, because there is a form of interviewing that requires little or no knowledge of the interviewee's particular situation. Consider the following hypothetical extract from a discussion about one Area of headship, 'external relations', focusing specifically upon the Aspect of 'governors'.

Head: 'I am concerned at the level of knowledge of some of the governors.'

Appraiser: 'Regarding?'

H: 'Oh, education generally, the recent reforms and the very real problems which this school faces.'

A: 'What sort of problems?'

H: 'Well, this authority has cut back more than most at a time when there is a growing teacher shortage and an increasing number of children with special needs. We are continually battling to get staff and are regularly operating with two or three teachers short. We have to make do with some pretty inexperienced cover.'

A: 'And you think that the governors do not understand this?'

H: 'Maybe some do but many just seem to adopt a critical attitude and can't or won't believe that my staff are working flat out and need their support.'

A: 'Do you think that their attitude could be changed?'

H: 'It is interesting that you ask that question because I was only discussing the same thing with the chair of governors last week, and he was mentioning a training package which he had heard about that might help.'

A: 'Yes?'

H: 'I have asked my deputy to contact County Hall about this.'

A: 'What else might be done?'

H: 'Well I was wondering . . .'

The important point about this snippet of conversation is that the appraiser asks only open, non-judgemental questions, all of which could be posed without prior information and knowledge concerning this particular situation and problem.

The approach adopted above, sometimes called non-directive interviewing, is much used in counselling and some forms of research interviewing. The aim is to help the respondents to identify and work through their own issues, concerns or problems and to work towards their own solutions. The interviewer acts more as a sounding board than as an expert. There are certain skills attached to this but the basic ones can be learned and applied quite quickly and effectively by appraisers (see Chapter 7).

The knowledge that at least part of the appraisal interview can be conducted using responsive questioning of this kind can be of considerable help to an appraiser who is worried about collecting information. There will always be limited time, probably a day or a day and a half at most, and it will therefore be impossible to collect all the information that the parties to the appraisal might wish. They will consequently be concerned to make the best use of the time available and to decide carefully upon their priorities during the initial meeting. This will be helped if they realize that some of their discussions can still be effective even if only one of them has information on the topic under review. That the person who possesses this knowledge will normally be the head suggests that he or she will be better prepared for the interview if some form of self-review has taken place beforehand. This is a matter dealt with later in this chapter.

Appraisal, however, is not counselling even if, occasionally, part of the discussion is conducted using a counselling style of questioning. More is necessary if, as suggested in Chapter 4, an 'outsider' is to assist the head in reviewing aims, plans and policies, discussing concerns about the school from whatever source they come and considering ways of improving the management of the school. In all of this the appraiser's role should involve bringing to the process the perspective of those with a relevant stake or interest in the school.

Clearly more information is necessary – but what kind of information? This is considered next.

The nature and sources of information for appraisal

Information in the present context includes numerical data, facts, perceptions, beliefs and opinions. There are five main sources of information, which are dealt with in turn: the appraisee's own knowledge; documents; observed situations; formal and informal interviews; and questionnaires. These were dealt with briefly in Chapter 4 and are now examined in greater depth.

The appraisee's own knowledge

The head, as senior manager, will normally possess considerable information about the school, especially if she or he has worked there for some time. But this information can be put to more effective use in the appraisal situation if the opportunity for careful reflection is taken. This can be helped and encouraged by the appraiser in two ways.

First, the head should be offered a *self-review pro forma* which requires answers to a number of questions. These questions will normally relate to the five Areas referred to in Chapter 4, i.e. the management and development of: teaching, learning and the curriculum; staff; finance and resources; external relations; and the head's own professional development. These Areas can be explained to the appraisee in the initial letter from the appraiser and the prompt list containing examples of Aspects associated with each of the Areas (see Chapter 4) will be enclosed with that letter.

Many types of questionnaire have been used in connection with teacher and headteacher appraisal and all have their advantages and disadvantages. Should they be long and contain a great many specific questions? Should they contain only a few open-ended questions? How much space should be allowed on the form for answers to each question? What seems to please some may not satisfy others. Those setting up appraisal schemes may feel it necessary to experiment with different forms.

One pro forma that has stood the test of time and generally seems to provide reasonable stimulus for thought and writing contains questions of the following kind.

1 What is your vision for the school over the coming years. In other words, despite the constraints you are likely to meet, how would you like the school to be in, say, five years time?
2 Consider the four areas of management – curriculum, staff, finance and physical resources and external relations, and with your school development plan in mind answer the following questions:
   (a) In which of these areas are you generally satisfied with your performance?
   (b) Can you give reasons why this is so?
   (c) In which have you experienced difficulty and would like developments to take place?
   (d) Can you say why this is so?
3 (a) Are there areas of your job that you find particularly demanding or stressful?
   (b) Can you give reasons why this is so?
   (c) Do you have any ideas as to what action you might take to alleviate some of the demands or stress?
4 What has been your main contribution to developing the school over the past year?
5 How do you see your own professional development over the next few years?

These are just a few of the possible questions that might be included in a self-evaluation pro forma. There are many more that could be asked and a full questionnaire of the type that has been used by the authors on several occasions is included as Appendix 1.

The form is best completed before the initial meeting since it will stimulate thinking about the head's role generally and also help to identify those Areas that might eventually form the focus of the appraisal. It is not expected that the completed form will be given to the appraiser: this will be entirely for the appraisee to decide. Whether it is shared or not, it will still provide a useful *aide-mémoire* during both the initial meeting and the main appraisal interview.

The head can also be encouraged to reflect in another way before the interview. During the initial meeting it could be suggested to the appraisee that he or she might like to write a *personal statement* to stimulate further thinking before the main interview. This statement could be based upon information or ideas stemming from discussions with colleagues, parents, governors etc.; it might be collected by the head as part of the agreed appraisal contract; or it could stem from writings in a journal, if one is kept by the head. It might contain reflections of further thoughts on, for instance:

- the head's vision for the school;
- the Areas and Aspects that will form the focus of the appraisal and that have been dealt with only briefly in the pro forma;
- possible targets that might be worked upon during the main interview;
- ideas on 'what I want from the appraisal'.

The statement will normally be for the head's own use, although it might be shared if he or she so wishes.

Documents

Annex A to Circular 12/91 considers that:

head teacher appraisers should be familiar with current national and, in LEA maintained schools, LEA policies and requirements with regard to curriculum, special needs, equal opportunities, staffing and cover, disciplinary and grievance procedures and other such matters relating to school management.

(para. 15)

There are therefore many documents which might provide useful background information including:

- the school prospectus or any information sent to parents;
- whole-school or curriculum policies and plans;
- governors' reports to parents;
- agendas or minutes of meetings and associated papers;
- reports following school inspections;
- documents containing figures on, for example, pupil performance, pupil numbers, absenteeism etc.

The list in paragraph 16 of Annex A to Circular 12/91 should also be referred to (see Appendix 3). In fact, any report, letter, statistical analysis or other document that might throw some light upon a particular Area or Aspect to be covered in the appraisal process might be of use.

As indicated above, it will be a matter for agreement as to whether such documents should all be available to the appraiser. It could well be the case that some information of this kind is confidential and, although of relevance to matters under review, should remain in the sole possession of the appraisee. No hard and fast rules can be made regarding this issue but it highlights the importance of the preliminary meeting and the contract that stems from it.

Observed situations

It is possible to gain a general impression of a school's atmosphere or climate by visiting briefly a number of classrooms and observing in the playground, corridors, staffroom or library at appropriate times. The preliminary discussion should have produced agreement about the arrangements for such visits, and whether the appraisee should observe in more detail the work of the school and, if so, exactly what would be looked at. There are various possibilities, including, for instance: the head at work, e.g. teaching, supervising or coaching staff, taking a seminar with students on practice, chairing meetings, hosting parents' evenings, contributing to governor's meetings etc.; engaging with other personnel at work, in classrooms, supervising extra-curricular events, staff meetings, parent–teacher association meetings etc.

The time factor is clearly a constraint on how much can be achieved in a day. Observation is also something that needs to be handled with care and sensitivity – a matter that is considered again later in this chapter. It should always be remembered that the reason for observing people or events in a head's appraisal is to gain greater knowledge and understanding of how she or he manages the school and of the form of action that might lead to improvements in the management of the Areas and Aspects that are the focus of the appraisal.

Formal and informal interviews

Within the inevitable time constraints, the appraiser may agree with the head to interview other staff, governors, parents, ancillary helpers, advisers and in some circumstances pupils or teachers in secondary schools who receive the pupils.

Anyone who might reasonably be expected to hold information or views about the working of the school will fall within the category of possible interviewee. But it need not necessarily be the appraiser who carries out such interviews. It might be agreed at the preliminary meeting that the head should undertake some of these, thus extending his or her knowledge of certain Areas or Aspects under review. Possibly another member of staff (e.g. a deputy or curriculum coordinator) might carry out interviews and report back to the head verbally or in writing. This all contributes to the process of obtaining information.

Questionnaires

While interviews are valuable for probing certain issues in depth, questionnaires are more useful for obtaining information from a broad cross-section of people. Thus, for instance, a questionnaire might be used to elicit parents' views on a specific aspect of external relations, such as home–school links. Provided that those seeking the information are satisfied with a limited response rate (a 20 or 30 per cent return is not unusual), questionnaires can add to the stock of information on specific matters. They might also be used with staff, pupils or certain community groups.

It is not necessary for the appraiser to be involved in the process although she or he may wish to help in drawing up the questions. The head or another member of staff could take responsibility for sending out and collecting in the forms, for analysing the data and for preparing a report.

Issues associated with the collection and use of information

In the previous two sections various problems and issues relating to information for appraisal emerged and there is little doubt, judging from the views of a great many participants in training workshops, that this is a matter which causes some concern. There are problems of deciding what information is necessary, of collecting it in the time available, of doing so diplomatically without causing upset or offence, of interpreting the information and giving it its due weight and, finally, of using it to good effect during the appraisal interview. There are thus logistic problems, ethical issues and the need for certain skills. Some of these have been alluded to in earlier discussions but it is proposed now to bring the various strands together in order to suggest some guidelines and practices that may help to make the problems more manageable.

Logistic problems

The Government will provide limited financial support for appraisal. The Secretary of State wrote to Chief Education Officers in December 1990 as follows:

Many of the things which need to be done for appraisal are there-fore already being done; appraisal is just a more systematic way of doing them. The only elements of operating costs which the Secretary of State considers it necessary to assist with in the introduction of the system are teacher substitution during observation and the costs of organising appraisal.

(DES, 1990a, para. 8)

Circular 12/91, paragraph 15 indicates the amount of grant available (£10 million) will be allocated in the 1991–2 financial year, a further £14 million in 1992–3 and similar levels in 1993–4 and 1994–5. Local authorities will no doubt apply for and receive grants according to a formula and will then provide limited 'cover' for those involved in the observational aspects of the appraisal process, mainly to release those who would otherwise be unable to leave their classroom. This will probably also apply to headteachers, particularly those with a full teaching load. But the amounts will not be large and it is unlikely when schemes are fully implemented that more than a day will be available for the collection of information.

Whatever decisions are made by LEAs regarding the allocation of funding, it is clear that the imposition of an appraisal scheme, which in any one year could involve heads in their own appraisal and possibly the appraisal of other heads, inevitably means that the time that can be devoted to the task must be strictly limited. It is therefore necessary to draw up a plan based upon carefully thought out priorities and to ensure that this plan is strictly adhered to. There are a number of ways of improving the chances of this happening.

Purpose of collecting information

The main purpose of data collection is to provide information regarding the head's management of the school. It is not an inspection, an evaluation or a whole-school review. It is primarily concerned with the way in which heads carry out their management responsibilities with regard to certain Areas and Aspects of their job. The information should therefore be related only to those Aspects that form the focus of the appraisal.

Contract

The preliminary meeting is organized to draw up a contract. The agreement reached will specify what information should be collected, about what, how and by whom. This is written down on a relatively short form (see Appendix 4) and the process of doing this should make it clear that collecting information is a strictly limited exercise. Areas and Aspects provide the focus. Feasibility is the key-word. Drawing up the detailed programme for the visit should rein-force the message that only a limited amount can be done in a day by the appraiser.

Sharing the load

It is not solely the appraiser's responsibility to collect information. The greater the number of people who can be involved in the process the more the load will be spread. There may also be advantages in involv-ing other staff. It may help them to identify with and support what is going on. They may come to realize that it could, and it is hoped should, benefit the school. They will see that the head is being appraised and this may encourage them to become committed to appraisal as a means of furthering their own development. And finally, the task of collecting information for the head's appraisal might, in certain circumstances, be regarded as a form of staff development for them.

Ethical issues

In general, those who possess, pass on, receive and otherwise deal with information will try to establish their own interpretations of what they see and hear. They are involved in a search for meaning. The 'truth' or the 'reality' of a situation is closely related to their attempts to make sense of the data they receive.

Information collected in the appraisal process is almost certain to be subjective to some degree and must be dealt with accordingly. Its relative weight, as far as 'truthfulness', reliability, relevance and usefulness for appraisal purposes is concerned, must always be care-fully considered. It may be necessary sometimes to exercise healthy scepticism or even to ignore information because of its source or the circumstances in which it is collected. Hearsay and rumour fall within this category. They may provide important background 'noise' for the appraiser but they should be used with extreme care, if at all, in formal appraisal discussions.

There can be no simple rules to formulate action with regard to ethics in this situation. Both appraiser and appraisee must, to a large extent, rely upon the mature professional judgement of the other. Ex-perience of headship is, in itself, a good grounding and there are few heads who have not learned some of the skills of diplomacy in their work with people. But it is possible to give some guidelines and re-minders that take into account the potential concerns and sensitivities of those who are involved in the process.

Informing staff

It is important to inform staff of the reason for the appraiser's visit and of what he or she will be doing in the school. What follows is a version of a letter that an appraisee head might send to all staff.

> I am about to engage in my annual appraisal. During this term my appraiser (insert name), another head from within the LEA, will be visiting the school and on 30 March will, with my full agreement, be talking to several people and observing various activities.
>
> This is to advise you that the visit is not a whole-school review but is concerned with my appraisal, which is similar in many ways to those that you have experienced for yourselves.
>
> It is possible that the appraiser may ask to speak to some of you, to see documents or to arrange to attend a meeting or other event at which you may be present. I would value your cooperation in is. May I also ask you to provide any information that will assist in the full discussion of matters in order to make the appraisal beneficial to me and to the school as a whole.
>
> It is not possible at this stage to say which staff will be involved but I will let you know as soon as I can. In the limited time available it will only be possible for the appraiser to see a few people but even if you are not involved it is important that you are aware of why he or she is in the school.
>
> There is now available a national code of practice regarding the collection of information for appraisal and, in case you have not seen this, a copy is attached.
>
> Thank you for your help.

The letter would of course be adapted to suit particular circumstances. Some heads may think it more appropriate to give the gist of the letter to staff during a meeting or to people individually. Either way, it is important that staff are aware of what is going on. A 'code of practice' is mentioned in the letter above the main points that might be embodied in this are now considered.

A code of practice

The following points are either quoted directly or adapted from the Guidance and code of practice which forms Annex A of Circular 12/91. The full Annex is set out in Appendix 3. (The numbers following each statement relate to paragraphs in the Annex.)

Procedural points

Neither appraisers nor appraisees should act in any way likely to threaten the trust and confidence upon which the appraisal is based. (11)

Interviews for the purpose of information collection should be held on a one-to-one basis. (7)

Any written statements should remain confidential to the author, the appraiser and the appraisee. (21)

Appraiser's responsibilities

The appraiser should be familiar with current national and LEA policies and requirements with regard to curriculum, special needs, equal opportunities, staffing and cover, disciplinary and grievance procedures and other matters relating to school management. (15)

She or he should also be familiar with the workings of the school as a result of reading documents provided by the appraisee head (16), including the head's job description if such exists. (14)

When interviewing people providing information the appraiser should explain the purpose of the interview and the way in which information will be treated. (19)

Appraisers should act with sensitivity to all concerned and not exhibit bias in collecting information. (4)

Those giving information should not be put under any pressure save that of relevance and accuracy. (5)

Any information received anonymously should not be used. (8)

Information that does not relate to the professional performance of the head should not be sought or accepted. (9)

Informant's responsibilities

General comments should be supported by specific examples. (6)

Informants should be encouraged to make fair and considered comments which they are prepared to acknowledge and substantiate if required. (20)

Those offering significantly critical comments should be asked to discuss them directly with the appraisee before they are used as appraisal information. (22)

Except where personal opinion is specifically asked for (as when an attempt is being made to gauge staff reaction to an innovation), care should be taken to ensure that information is sought and presented in an objective way. (23)

These guidelines set out a desired state of affairs which may not always be easily reached. Nevertheless, they exist to assist in the building and maintaining of trust and confidence and attempts to put them into practice should help to reduce both anxiety and misunderstandings that might otherwise occur.

The skills of collecting information for appraisal

Some of the skills of collecting information have already been mentioned in the preceding two sections. There are, for instance, the skills asssociated with planning a visit to the appraisee's school and using the time to best effect. There are also the skills of diplomacy related to understanding and observing an ethical code of practice as outlined above. But what have not been mentioned so far are the particular research skills necessary to collect and analyse information from interviews, observation, questionnaires and documents. There is an additional skill of providing constructive feedback to an appraisee using the information obtained.

Where might appraisers obtain these skills? It is possible that some heads might have acquired them as a result of further study for an advanced diploma or higher degree in education. Others may have learned some or all of them on LEA courses covering school review, classroom observation or evaluation. Many may have practised interviewing and feedback skills while attending training programmes for teacher review or appraisal.

There may well exist, therefore, a repository of such skills among appraiser heads. But this cannot be assumed and it is necessary to consider training for headteacher appraisal based upon an analysis of their needs. It should be possible to organize a programme that provides for group discussion and practice and also for some individualized learning using guided reading, distance learning and paired practice. This is discussed in more detail in Chapter 7.

Summary

In this chapter the nature and sources of information for appraisal were considered. It was suggested that these could be grouped under five main headings: the appraisee's own knowledge, documents, observed situations, formal and informal interviews and questionnaires. These were discussed in turn. The collection of information from each of these sources is not without its problems and these were identified as: logistic (finding the time and organizing a programme to obtain information), ethical (requiring diplomacy and sensitivity to the needs and concerns of those involved) and research skills (needed for interviewing, observation, using questionnaires etc). Ways of managing these problems were suggested and a code of practice was described.

_____ 6

_____ *The appraisal interview*

We use the term 'interview' here to refer to the main, formal meeting (following the collection of information) between the head and the two appraisers – the appraiser head and the adviser. Some heads prefer the term 'discussion' rather than interview for the reason that it suggests shared responsibilities and a more evenly balanced exchange of views. Interview, by contrast, holds connotations of interrogation and one-sided questioning and probing. But the nature of an interview can vary and can just as well take the form of a caring, stimulating encounter geared towards the opening up and exploration of key issues by the appraisee, with the appraiser mainly listening and guiding the meeting through its various stages. An interview of this kind will contain discussion but the control of the process, based upon an agreed agenda and ground rules, will remain largely with the appraiser head. In these circumstances the term 'interview' seems more appropriate.

The place and purpose of the interview in the appraisal process

Although the interview is sometimes thought of as the essence of the appraisal it will have become clear from earlier chapters that it is but a small, if important, part of the whole process. It is normally preceded by: preliminary contact between the appraiser head and the appraisee; the completion of a self-evaluation form and reflection by the appraisee; and an initial meeting followed by the collection of information, which will normally involve a visit, observation and interviews in the school by the appraiser head.

The interview is followed by the writing of an agreed report or statement, action towards achieving targets and a follow-up meeting about a year later between the appraiser and appraisee to consider progress. Subsequently, the next cycle of appraisal, building upon the first, will begin.

The purpose of the interview is to provide the opportunity for the appraisers and appraisee to meet for an uninterrupted period to cover an agenda dealing with those matters that they have agreed are important for improving the management of the school and the head's own professional development. In the interview situation the appraisers will demonstrate, through questioning, listening and support, the stance of objective outsiders representing the views of those who have an interest in the school and the way it is managed.

With this purpose and the role of the appraisers in mind there are various aspects of the interview that need to be considered. These are the:

- agenda and ground rules;
- structure of the interview;
- skills of the interviewer;
- desired outcomes;
- interview statement;
- identification of targets;
- follow-up meeting.

These are dealt with in turn.

Agenda and ground rules

Why have an agenda and ground rules? The answer to this question has largely been dealt with in Chapters 4 and 5 but it is worth bringing together the various points in order to stress the importance of these factors.

First, there is the matter of building trust and confidence. If the appraisal is to be truly developmental the appraisee must trust the intentions and professional skills of the appraiser. This is helped if both parties are clear about exactly what is meant to happen and how it is to take place. The initial meeting (Chapter 4) and the contract, which is agreed at that discussion and sets out some ground rules, are all part of this process.

Second, as part of the contract Areas for review and Aspects of

those Areas that will provide the focus for the appraisal were identified. These Areas and Aspects, including the head's own professional
development, will form the basis for the agenda. Once set, the agenda
will help to structure and set the boundaries of the interview.

Third, an agenda is necessary because of the limited time available
for the interview. There may be some flexibility but normally it will
not be expected that the interview will take more than two, or at most
three, hours. Only if all the matters to be covered are clearly set out
beforehand can the possibility of spending too long on some items and
little, or even none, on others be attended to.

What kinds of ground rules are necessary?

An important ground rule already alluded to is that it is not acceptable for either party to introduce new issues that are not on the agenda
once the interview is underway. This is necessary both to maintain
trust and confidence and also to ensure that all items are covered. If an
issue does arise during the interview which is not on the agenda but
which seems to both parties to be important it could be noted and
referred to after the formal interview has ended. A decision may then
be made on how best to deal with it.

A second ground rule concerns confidentiality. Anything that is
discussed during the interview should be entirely confidential. Only
those matters set out in the appraisal statement, and agreed by both
parties, relating to targets for action may be referred to outside the
meeting.

A third ground rule refers to the role of appraiser heads. It will
normally be the case that they will, in effect, chair the meeting, especially with regard to keeping to time and covering the agenda.

A fourth rule that it is useful to establish before the meeting for-
mally starts concerns the keeping of notes. It is normally assumed that
the appraiser will keep notes but the reasons for this are worth clarifying. Notes may be necessary at various points during the interview to
help the appraiser to summarize what has been said up to that point –
perhaps to end one part of the discussion before moving on to the next
or to bring the meeting to a close. They are also useful as an *aide-
mémoire* for writing the statement and setting targets. There may also
be advantages in the appraisee taking notes. This is not only useful for
jointly verifying points made earlier but can even up the flow of the
interview by creating short breaks as both parties pause to write.
There is a sense in which authority and accountability within the interview are more equally spread as a result of the mutual commitment to
listening carefully that writing notes demand.

Finally, although it may seem an obvious point, the time for the
interview should be regarded as sacrosanct and interruptions from any

source should be avoided. It may seem sensible, if two or more hours have been set aside for the discussion, to plan a break either at an agreed time or when a certain point in the agenda has been reached.

Structure of the interview

The meeting will normally begin with agreement of the agenda. Some appraisers prefer to save time by discussing this by telephone beforehand or even writing to the appraisee setting out a draft agenda after visiting the school to collect information. Either way, some time will still be necessary before the formal interview begins.

The agenda will provide a general structure for the interview but this raises two questions: where do agenda items come from, and how should they be ordered and structured?

Where do agenda items come from?

The first question is to some extent answered in Chapter 4, in which Areas and Aspects for appraisal were discussed. These provide the main source for the agenda. Thus, in Chapter 4 the example of one Area – 'management and development of staff' – was suggested and sub-divided into several Aspects. If within this Area the agreed focus for the appraisal was specifically 'staff development' then certain Aspects might be chosen, such as: the effectiveness of the staff development committee; the place of the staff development policy in school life; perceptions of staff about the current priorities and programme; and the views of staff regarding satisfaction of their personal needs. It would then be quite possible to make staff development one section of the interview and to work through the four Aspects one at a time. The other agreed Area for review (e.g. 'external relations') and the head's own professional development would then follow and the structure of the interview, as determined by the agenda, might be as here:

Possible format A
Item 1. Management of staff development. A review of agreed Aspects.
Item 2. External relations. A review of agreed aspects.
Item 3. Professional development. A review of agreed Aspects.
Item 4. Further action, meetings etc.

There is more to structuring an interview than setting out agreed agenda items and this raises the second question referred to above.

How should the agenda items be ordered and structured?

Within any Area or Aspect that forms the focus for an agenda item there are various matters that may require attention. The completed self-evaluation pro forma, for instance, may well have raised the matter of satisfaction set against the need for further development and both may need to be discussed.

Running through all the items is the temporal factor – past, present and future. How much of the interview should be devoted to each? Dwelling on past performance, for instance, may be necessary in some cases but could be psychologically bad in others. It may be useful to dwell on the present for a time but there are usually good grounds for looking forward and considering what action may be necessary in the future.

There is also the matter of targets, which can take a great deal of time to agree in detail. How much detail is it necessary to complete during the interview itself? Should targets be dealt with within the Area or Aspect under review or should target-setting be left until the end of the interview? (These questions are discussed in more detail later under the heading 'Targets'.)

Finally, there are often points of procedure, factual matters and timing to be dealt with, all of which may contribute to the settling down or 'putting at ease' process.

These are all structural matters that have to be addressed by the three parties in considering the agenda. Depending upon how they are resolved, there are several possible formats that could be adopted in addition to format A above.

Possible format B
Item 1. Establishing procedures and ground rules. Clarifying factual matters. Ordering items and setting estimated time limits.
Item 2. Matters giving rise to satisfaction in those Areas under review.
Item 3. Areas where it is felt that further improvements/developments might be made.
Item 4. Professional development, including career review.
Item 5. Targets arising from items 3 and 4.
Item 6. Further action, meetings etc.

An alternative structure might be as follows.

Possible format C
Item 1. Establishing procedures and ground rules. Clarifying factual matters. Ordering items and setting estimated time limits.

Item 2. Management of staff development. Areas of satisfaction. Areas where improvement/development is desirable. Targets arising.
Item 3. Management of external relations. Areas of satisfaction. Areas where improvement/development is desirable. Targets arising.
Item 4. Professional development. Career review. Targets arising.
Item 5. Further action, meetings etc.

A further possible format using the temporal dimension might be

Possible format D
Item 1. Establishing procedures and ground rules. Clarifying factual matters. Setting priorities and estimated time limits.
Item 2. A general discussion of performance over the past two or three years in the Areas agreed for appraisal, noting feelings of satisfaction and dissatisfaction in relation to them.
Item 3. Where are we now? A consideration of the present situation with regard to the Areas under review. To include professional development.
Item 4. The future. A discussion of the head's vision for the school. Setting targets for moving towards this vision in the agreed Areas.
Item 5. Further action, meetings etc.

Finally, it may be seen as important that a head with a substantial teaching load should include teaching as a part of the interview.

Possible format E
Item 1. Establishing procedures and ground rules. Clarifying factual matters. Setting priorities and estimated time limits.
Item 2. The head as teacher – strengths and aspects of the work where support and development are appropriate.
Item 3. The head as manager – Areas and Aspects agreed for review including Areas of satisfaction and Areas where improvement and/or development is desirable. Targets arising.
Item 4. Professional development. Career review. Targets arising.
Item 5. Further action, meetings etc.

There are other possible combinations of factors that might be used to create a format and it is not possible to recommend any one in particular. Some appraisers and appraisees will feel comfortable with one approach, some with another. Much depends upon circumstances and preferred style. Indeed, experience over a number of years may lead to a flexible approach with the possibility of using any of the formats or even a less formal, partially intuitive approach, if this seems to work for some. To begin with though, especially when attempting to build trust and confidence, it would seem sensible to pick what seems to be a feasible, comfortable structure and to stay with it for the duration of the interview.

The skills of the interviewers

The skills needed by the interviewers are those necessary to fulfil the appraisers' role as stated earlier, namely to assist the head to: explore her or his vision for the school; review relevant aims, plans and policies; identify and discuss concerns about the school from whatever source they come; consider ways of improving the management of the school; set targets for the coming year; and, generally, to provide feedback, support and encouragement. To achieve the aim implicit in this role, the interviewers, and particularly the appraiser head, will need to balance potentially competing elements of the role.

Controlling and directing versus attending and counselling skills

Controlling and directing skills are necessary where an agenda must be covered with a finite time span. The interviewer is, in effect, chairing a meeting and carries the responsibility of ensuring that the ground rules are observed and that the meeting reaches a satisfactory conclusion as far as the agenda and rules are concerned. The task may involve dealing with silences, handling criticism, dealing with sensitive issues in a fair and open way, using information gained during the visit appropriately and diplomatically, eliciting and incorporating contributions from an adviser, moving from discussion to targets and helping to set realistic targets.

Attending and counselling skills, by contrast, involve the art of listening and helping the appraisee to talk openly and honestly about the Areas of work under review, as well as matters connected with professional development. This means creating space, adopting a low profile, using carefully chosen questions, and paraphrasing and summarizing well, to assist the appraisee in thinking through ideas, progress and problems. These skills are, in effect, akin to those of a client-centred counsellor.

The skills of the counsellor and the controller are brought together in the interview by moving from one to the other as appropriate. Attending skills may give way to directing skills when the interviewer judges that it is the right time to move on to the next item on the agenda. Indeed, it may be useful to explain this dual role to the appraisee beforehand. Ideally it is a matter that should be raised in any appraisal training scheme (see Chapter 7).

Supporting and encouraging versus probing and challenging skills

The second dimension indicates, at the extreme, the potential distinction between the 'cosiness' of total, unquestioning acceptance on the one hand and an inquisitive interventionist style on the other. The balance, which is not always easy to attain, will stretch, stimulate and challenge the appraisee while still enabling him or her to feel secure and supported.

The appraiser, therefore, must walk a difficult path in order to establish and maintain an appropriate balance throughout the interview. Clearly, as well as training in these skills, experience will help considerably in building the understanding and sensitivity necessary for the task.

Desired outcomes

An activity often used in training workshops is to ask those about to be appraised in a practice situation what, if the interview was real, they would like to achieve as a result of it. Following the interview they are again asked what was achieved and despite the fact that it was a practice interview there is often a considerable overlap between the before and after statements. An analysis of the statements made in workshops spanning several years suggests that there is a great deal of commonality in what appraisees want from an interview. Furthermore, these desired outcomes are not dissimilar from what LEAs or government would hope to achieve by the introduction of an appraisal system.

They can be categorized under three headings: challenge, clarity and confidence.

Challenge

Appraisees want to be challenged. They point out that they are investing a great deal of time, thought and emotional energy in the appraisal process and they do not want to waste them on 'cosseting', as one person put it.

Those about to be interviewed suggest such phrases as 'friendly pushing', 'professional probing', 'sensitive but firm questioning'. 'I want to be made to see my blindspots.' 'I don't want to be let off the hook in areas I seem to avoid.' They hope that the appraiser will act like a professional colleague but not a timid or soft one. He or she should know what the job is about from experience and should be able to see through any 'smokescreen' put up by the appraisee. Those about to be interviewed are prepared to be 'pushed' in this way because they know that it is the way to learn and develop.

Confidence

Challenge is one thing, building confidence is another. Some appraisees compare the process to helping children to learn. 'You can push too far and destroy their confidence and that can be a disaster.'

Those interviewed want to leave the room feeling that their appraiser has understood and respected them and has helped them to feel more, rather than less, confident to carry on and develop in their job. Maintaining the balance between challenge and confidence-building is a sensitive process and requires skills of a high order. As one appraiser put it, 'it is like walking on eggshells'.

The shattering of an appraisee's confidence could have far-reaching effects, and is not what the Government, LEAs or individuals want. Confidence does not imply smugness; rather it means a sense of having been challenged in terms of a review of one's work and of having come out with a better understanding of what has to be done and how to do it. This links with the next desired outcome – clarity.

Clarity

Appraisees want to come out of the interview with a clearer sense of what their job is about, now and in the future. If there is a job description, then they would expect it to play some part in the discussions. If not, then the Areas and Aspects chosen for review ought to provide the framework for probing into the tasks involved and the problems and possibilities associated with them.

The appraisal interview provides an opportunity to stand back and, with the help of an outsider, begin to see the job in context and gain a new perspective on the nature of the work and how it is changing. Things that were done, or taken for granted, in the past may no longer be relevant in current conditions. New demands for change, in say curriculum or organization, may require old practices to be dropped and new ones, not yet thought about, to be planned and implemented. If the appraisal is to be effective then the head will want to feel, at the end of the interview, able to move forward with a sense of priority and direction in dealing with the necessary changes. In this respect 'targets' are important and these are dealt with next.

Targets

A target is a statement of intent agreed by two or more people. It refers to a desired state of affairs to be achieved in the future. In most circumstances it will concern change resulting in improvement of some kind.

Targets should bring together the three desired outcomes referred to above – challenge, confidence and clarity. To achieve this they require certain ingredients. A target should:

1 *Specify a goal* that is *attainable*, but that requires the head to engage in activities over and above those of a routine nature which would have been undertaken in the normal course of events. Often such goals have previously been thought about in vague terms (e.g. 'to do something about assemblies, school trips, staff meetings') but need the discipline of a target to bring them to the point of action.

2 Be *specific* rather than general. 'To improve my management skills' is too general for a target. 'To become better at delegating tasks to my deputy' is more specific and can be made into a target.

3 Be *appropriate and relevant* for the development of the school and/ or the head at that time. This is a motivational point. There is little benefit to be obtained from setting targets merely for the sake of setting them. The head needs to feel that they are important and will make a difference to the way the school is managed. For this reason the idea for a target should ideally come from the appraisee rather than the appraiser. There is then more likely to be a sense of ownership and commitment. The appraiser's role should be to help to clarify goals and focus on the action necessary to achieve them.

4 Be feasible within the *time scale* set. Time is an important factor. The vague hope of completing something in the future is not satisfactory for a target. Once firm dates are brought on to the agenda (e.g. to report to the governors by 25 March) the feasibility, or otherwise, of the target is made clear.

5 Specify the *action to be taken* to achieve the agreed goal. A discussion of the action necessary will again indicate whether the target is feasible or not. The appraisee may well decide after the interview to draw up a detailed action plan but for the purpose of writing up the target for the appraisal statement (see later) a series of action steps accompanied by dates is normally sufficient.

6 Specify *criteria for success*. If the target focused upon, say, 'improving skills of delegation' then how would the head or anyone else know that improvement had taken place? A target should, therefore, contain a statement that suggests ways in which the achievement of the target can be verified. If, for instance, the target referred

to the head delegating more managerial tasks to the deputy, then it might be possible at the end of the allotted time period for the head and deputy to review what had been achieved in this respect and to assess its impact upon the work of the school. A date might be included in the target for this meeting to take place.

Levels of target

Targets set by heads will relate to their role in managing – the whole school, groups or individuals within it or their own professional development – and the nature of the target will reflect this. Some targets may span all three.

At whole-school level, for instance, the target may relate to how the head manages the setting up and carrying out of a review (e.g. of part of the curriculum or of parental involvement in school matters). At the level of groups or individuals targets may be connected with, say, the head's strategy for managing the improvement of reception procedures for infants, involving the three teachers most concerned. Or it may relate to coaching a deputy in order to enable him to deal with in-school budget allocations in the future. Finally, the target may be concerned with ways in which the head might improve his or her own skills or practices, such as making more time to focus on planning and policy-making.

The example in Figure 6.1 illustrates the wording of a target at whole-school level. It contains a detailed action plan, which the appraisee might well write up after the interview. Not all targets can be planned in so much detail in advance but this example is set out in full to illustrate what can be done in certain instances. The time needed to do this should not be underestimated.

Another type of target concerned with the head's own professional development is suggested in Figure 6.2.

Targets such as those in Figures 6.1 and 6.2, or a summary of them, will normally appear in the appraisal statement (considered next) and be discussed by the appraiser and appraisee in the follow-up interview (see later part of this chapter).

The appraisal statement

A written statement is expected following the interview. But how long and detailed should it be, who should write it, where should it be kept, who should have access to it, for what purposes and how long should it be kept? These are just some of the questions that concern both appraisers and appraisees.

Target

To improve monitoring of the science curriculum in action

Action

1   Reading. Identify and read documents concerning curriculum monitoring. Check possibilities with County INSET Adviser and with Education Department at university. Complete read/scan by end of March.

2   Discussions. Talk to deputy and science coordinator to ascertain their views on what is happening regarding monitoring the science curriculum at present. Ask them to discuss the matter with all staff involved and report back by the end of April. Pass on any useful readings to them both.

3   Staff development. Programme a half-day meeting on the topic for all staff at the next professional day in May. Objective: to draw up preliminary guidelines for a policy regarding monitoring the curriculum in science.

4   Policy preparation. Acquaint science coordinator with key features of policy construction and provide a detailed briefing for the task. A draft policy statement to be available by the end of June. Final draft to be presented to staff for comment at last staff meeting of the summer term.

5   Implementation. At the above meeting, make arrangements for implementation in the Autumn term. All staff involved to be briefed by the coordinator regarding the action they will be expected to take.

6   Evaluate. Coordinator to report back to the deputy and myself on the effectiveness of the scheme by the end of December. Discuss with both and obtain feedback on their perception of my management of the process and whether they would have preferred more or less guidance from me.

Figure 6.1   A whole-school level target.

Target

To provide for myself three hours per week of uninterrupted school time for planning, policy-making and focused discussions with relevant staff.

Action

From 6 January, keep time log for three weeks. Identify parts of the day when time might be found. Consider whether diary might be 'blocked' for one morning.

Discuss with school secretary. Consider feasibility of an appointment system and improved telephone facilities between offices.

Explain proposed plan to staff and ask for their cooperation.

Implement plan for remainder of the term. Write in diary how the 'blocked' time was used each day. Secretary and deputy to note occasions when my unavailability caused problems.

Review at end of the term with secretary and deputy, and continue or modify as appropriate.

Figure 6.2   A target for the headteacher's professional development.

There are now some fairly specific answers to these questions but there are also some problems. The guidelines relating to appraisal statements contained in *School Teacher Appraisal: a National Framework* (NSG, 1989) provide detailed guidance on most of the above issues but the Government response to this report (DES, 1991) does not coincide on certain key points, especially concerning access to and purposes for which the document may be used.

The NSG report, anticipating a DES Circular containing regulations, suggests the following principles and procedures with regard to appraisal statements for teachers. It is suggested in the report that there should be similar regulations for headteachers.

We recommend that the Regulations specify that after each

appraisal interview an appraisal statement should be prepared by the appraiser(s), in consultation with the appraisee, recording the main points made in discussion and the conclusions reached, including agreed targets. The Circular should indicate that the appraisee should be permitted to record separate comments if he or she wishes, either in the statement or separately, for example where the appraiser(s) and appraisee disagree over a particular point. It should also recommend that both appraiser(s) and appraisee be invited to indicate that they are content with the statement . . .

The Circular should indicate that targets for professional development and training should also be recorded in a separate note, which should also be agreed between the appraiser(s) and the appraisee. Where appropriate this note should be forwarded to those responsible for planning training and development at LEA and school level . . .

We take the firm view that access to appraisal statements should be restricted to the appraisee, the appraiser(s), the head teacher of the school, the CEO of the LEA and any LEA officer or adviser specifically designated by him or her. This restriction should apply to the use of statements by the appraisees as well as others . . . and the Circular should indicate that in the case of head teachers one copy of the statement should always be sent to the CEO . . .

The Circular should indicate that proposals for action deriving from appraisal should be reported to the governing body of the school if they require an executive decision by that body, or if they relate to the use of resources for which the governing body has specific, direct responsibility.

The circular should indicate that once an appraisal statement and any separate note on training and development has been agreed all other documents relevant to the appraisal should be destroyed. It should recommend that the period for which appraisal statements should remain on file is clearly established by LEAs, in consultation with teachers through the normal consultative machinery. We believe that it would normally be sensible to retain statements on files for the equivalent of two appraisal cycles.

(NSG, 1989, paras 63–7)

The initial response by the then Secretary of State, John MacGregor, was contained in a conference speech made on 14 September 1990 (MacGregor, 1990). In this, the recommendations of the NDC report were largely welcomed although the decision not to make Regulations obligatory was also made known. In October 1990 a document containing a draft National Framework and supplementary guidance was sent to CEOs and other interested parties for comment. This, apart from some abbreviated sections and the important modifications referred to next, was similar to the NSG report on appraisal statements.

Appraisal shall be an integral part of the management and support of teachers, and not an isolated exercise. It shall be clearly separated from disciplinary procedures. These procedures may, however, draw on relevant information from appraisal records, where appropriate. Information from appraisal records may also be taken into account, along with other factors, in decisions about promotions, and the pay of individual teachers.

(DES, 1990a, para. 3)

After a period of consultation the Circular and Regulations were produced in July 1991 and made clear that the Government intended to maintain some links between pay, promotion and discipline. The relevant paragraphs in the regulations are as follows:

13 – (2) In the case of a head teacher –
   (a)   the appraisers shall provide a copy of the appraisal statement to the chairman of the governing body of the school and, in the case of the head teacher of a school maintained by a local authority, to the Chief Education Officer or any officer or adviser to the authority specifically designated by the Chief Education Officer;
14 – (1)
Relevant information from appraisal records may be taken into account by head teachers, Chief Education Officers or any officers or advisers specifically designated by a Chief Education Officer . . . in advising those responsible for taking decisions on the promotion, dismissal or discipline of school teachers or on the use of any discretion in relation to pay.

The Circular also contains statements which although referring to school teachers are clearly of relevance to headteachers as well:

68. Appraisal should clearly be separate from disciplinary procedures: these separate procedures should be used where the school teacher's continuing employment or any other form of disciplinary offence is at issue. In disciplinary procedures, persons entitled to access to appraisal records may draw on relevant information from them, where appropriate, in line with regulation 14.

70. There will be no direct or automatic link between appraisal and promotion or additions to salary. But it is legitimate and desirable for head teachers to take into account information from appraisals along with other relevant information, in advising governors on promotions and pay.

It remains to be seen exactly how these regulations will work in practice. The link between appraisal and pay and conditions has always been a controversial one and until the recent DES statements it was assumed by many that the two would remain quite separate and distinct. But there has always been a view held by those who have organized and practised appraisal that, despite good intentions, it is impossible entirely to separate one management procedure – appraisal – from others such as discipline, motivation and reward. What is learned by someone during the appraisal process can hardly be forgotten if he or she then becomes involved in making decisions about, say, promotion. The problem is made more acute, especially for those who write and agree appraisal statements, if they know that the document might be referred to by those who have discipline, grievance procedures or pay and promotion decisions in mind. This will inevitably affect what is written in the statement.

The second issue arises from the possibility of governors having access to the statement. The NSG report recommended that

proposals for action deriving from appraisal should be reported to the governing body of the school if they require an executive decision by that body, or if they relate to the use of resources for which the governing body has specific, direct responsibility.

The Government's response (DES, 1990b) goes further: 'The appraisers shall send copies of the appraisal statement to the chairman of the governing body of the school and to the headteacher himself.'

Thus the whole statement, and not just those matters that require action by the governing body, will become available to the chair of governors. Many heads will not be concerned about this but others undoubtedly will. Again it raises the question of what should be included in the statement. The NSG guidelines provide some help. The report suggests that 'the main points made in discussion and the conclusions reached, including agreed targets' should be recorded and that 'targets for professional development and training should also be recorded in a separate note.'

These recommendations are confirmed in the Government's response. Essentially, therefore, the statement has to deal with (1) main points, (2) conclusions, (3) targets and (4) targets specifically related to

Appraisal statement

Appraisee _____

Appraiser _____

Adviser _____

Date of interview _____

Focus of appraisal

> Curriculum management
> – External relations
> Professional development

Curriculum management
The implementation of a policy for teaching and learning and the good start made in applying it in science, maths and English was acknowledged. It was agreed that attention should now be given to monitoring the policy in action (target 1). The valuable work of incentive allowance holders in science and topic work was considered and it was agreed that with the help of the head they should be encouraged to lead workshops for other staff with curriculum responsibilities. Opportunities should also be made for them to explain their work to the governors in the autumn term (target 2).

External relations
Parent–teacher consultation was identified as an area where developments were possible. The existing pilot scheme aimed at informing first-year parents about curriculum matters and pupil progress should be extended to second-year classes (target 3). An 'adopt a class' scheme to encourage governors to take a more active role should be explored (target 4).

Professional development
The head regarded recent curriculum initiatives as challenging. LMS (local management of schools) and budget strategies were also regarded as areas where further planning and policy-making were necessary. To achieve this the need for improved time management was regarded as essential. The possibility of creating 'quality' time for policy-making and discussions with other staff will be investigated

(target 5). The possibility of participating in the LEA Management Development in the School programme for heads and deputies is also to be actively pursued (target 6).

Targets – summary
1 To organize, with deputy, classroom observation for monitoring the implementation of teaching and learning policies in science initially and maths and English later (spring, summer and autumn terms).
2 To work with coordinators to arrange workshops for the rest of the staff (summer term). Arrange meeting between coordinators and governors regarding curriculum policies (summer term).
3 To organize a pilot project for teacher–parent liaison on curriculum and pupil progress (summer and autumn terms).
4 To explore an 'adopt a class' strategy. Raise at next staff meeting and discuss with chair of governors.
5 To introduce a strategy for creating blocks of uninterrupted time for head to deal with planning and complex matters.
6 To apply for the LEA four-day residential course on marketing and resource management.

Signed _____ (Reviewee)

        _____ (Reviewer)

        _____ (Adviser)

Figure 6.3 An example appraisal statement.

professional development and training, which should be recorded in a separate note (because this might have implications for resources). These requirements do not seem to imply a long and detailed document. Rather, they suggest something more along the lines of the minutes of a meeting, which can be quite short. If this is the case and if the document is one that is negotiated and agreed to by all parties there need be far less reason for anxiety about access and use of the document.

In various training workshops, draft appraisal statements have been produced and discussed by participants. Figure 6.3 shows one such example and illustrates the kind of report that should satisfy the national requirements.

The statement is short and covers key matters, conclusions and targets. It points to areas where development is necessary without criticizing the head or the management of the school. The targets are clearly stated and can be easily referred to again in the follow-up meeting.

The targets are best written out in more detail *after* the interview to create an action plan. The example of a detailed target regarding 'monitoring the curriculum' set out in Figure 6.1 illustrates how this might be done by the appraisee. This target is one that may well require further discussion with the governors since it may have re- source implications.

The follow-up interview

Both the National Framework (NSG, 1989) and the Government's responses (DES, 1990a, b; 1991) are clear and concise regarding the need for a follow-up interview. The latest document states: 'In the second year of the cycle, the appraiser(s) and appraisee shall meet to review the appraisal statement and progress in achieving agreed targets.'

Agreement between the parties would be necessary for setting a date but there would generally be no need for a preliminary meeting to agree an agenda, as in the main interview. The main purpose of the meeting is to consider the progress made in relation to agreed targets and possibly to modify them (if not achieved) or to set sub-targets in the light of experience over the year. It might also be possible to agree tentatively the Areas for review in the next appraisal cycle.

The supportive approach adopted in the main interview would con- tinue and the aims – to challenge, to build confidence and to achieve greater clarity regarding the job – would remain the key desirable outcomes. A brief summary statement would also be produced follow- ing the interview and would be attached to the original, thereby keep- ing an ongoing record of formal meetings.

Summary

The interview provides the opportunity for the appraiser(s) and appraisee to meet for an uninterrupted period to deal with those mat- ters that have previously been agreed to be important for improving the management of the school and the head's own professional development.

Before the interview the parties will agree ground rules (concerning such matters as note-taking and confidentiality) and an agenda. The agenda, normally based upon the agreed Areas and Aspects for review, will determine the structure of the interview.

Three outcomes are desirable. Within an atmosphere of trust and support the appraisers should attempt to: challenge the appraisee through the use of probing questions; help to build confidence; and clarify the role to be performed and the key tasks associated with it.

Targets represent the action element of the desired outcomes. They should set agreed goals and be specific, feasible, appropriate and relevant for the head and the school at the time. They should also contain criteria by which success can be judged.

An appraisal statement is required following an interview. It should, according to national guidelines, note the main points of the discussion and the conclusions reached and specify the targets. It should be agreed and signed by the parties to the interview. It is envisaged that the report will be short, no more than a page or two. There is concern about who should have access to the document and for what purposes. These questions should be answered through consultation at a national level in the future.

The follow-up interview will normally take place about one year after the main interview. It will be conducted on the lines of the earlier interview and seek to provide a challenge, build confidence and achieve greater role clarity. Its main purpose will be to review progress towards targets and consider what further action might be necessary to achieve them.

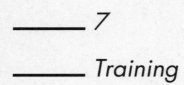

7

Training

In this chapter the question of training for appraisers and appraisees is addressed. The issues and problems likely to face LEAs in planning and providing a training programme are discussed first, followed by suggestions as to how such training might best be organized.

Issues for organizers

There are several issues that face organizers in providing training for headteacher appraisal. They are: possible content; training needs of participants; balance between information and practice; and time and costs. Each requires careful consideration since the solutions to the problems they raise will affect the nature of the training programme provided.

Content areas for training

Training for appraisal will normally require attention to six broad areas of content. These are:

1 The system to be adopted. This refers to questions concerning the length of the appraisal cycle, who appraises whom, the components of the cycle, such as interviews, documentation etc., and the order of events. Participants will require knowledge of national guidelines and the LEA's interpretation of them.

2 Purposes of appraisal. This is concerned with what the scheme

hopes to achieve. What should be the key aim or aims? Participants will need to have an understanding of the philosophy that guides the process and to appreciate what this means in practice.

3 The contract. The notion that a form of contract underpins the system and that careful negotiation is necessary to agree this and make it explicit must be understood by those taking part. They will require knowledge of the Areas of headship that might be considered and the need to focus on certain Areas and Aspects of the head's role.

4 Collection of information. The assumption is that appraisal will be more effective if the parties to it have adequate and appropriate information. But what is appropriate information and how might it be collected? In practice, agreement regarding the collection of information will become part of the contract referred to in point 3 and will require that participants have knowledge of research methods as well as some diplomatic skills.

5 The appraisal interview. The way in which the main appraisal meeting is conducted can have far-reaching effects on the outcomes of the entire process. Those conducting the interview will need to know how to structure the interview and must have the ability to listen, question and control the procedures.

6 Targets and appraisal statements. Appraisers should be able to help appraisees to identify possible targets and to define precisely what action will be necessary in order to achieve them. They will also need to write, or assist in writing, an appraisal statement embodying agreed targets. This will require negotiating and reporting skills.

Many of the matters mentioned above were covered in earlier parts of this book but their training implications are discussed later in this chapter in relation to the construction of training programmes.

Training needs of participants

The content areas referred to above provide a broad basis for training in appraisal skills and would normally be necessary for those about to embark upon teacher appraisal for the first time. But many heads will already have carried out appraisals (or development interviews) with their own staff and may have had some training in this connection. Consequently, some of the content may already have been covered. Furthermore, interviewing skills and those research skills necessary for collecting information could well have been dealt with in LEA, university, polytechnic or college courses connected with evaluation or classroom observation.

It is, therefore, difficult to predict, in general terms, what kind of

training appraisers will require. This will clearly differ within and be-
tweeen LEAs depending upon earlier training programmes. For this
reason it is important to consult heads, possibly through a survey using
a questionnaire and/or by means of a heads' representative group. If a
representative group already exists, or is set up for this purpose, it is
recommended that members take part in planning and implementing
the training programme. In one LEA where this happened the group
decided that, as the majority of heads in the county had already received training for appraising teachers, interview practice, which normally takes a considerable time, need not be included in the
programme.

There is also the question of appraisees' need for training. This has
been the subject of some debate. Since the ACAS agreement in 1986
(see Chapter 1) there has been an assumption that teachers about to
be appraised should receive some training, but recent pronouncements
by the Secretary of State seem to cast doubt upon the Government's
willingness to support this view. Further, it might be argued by some
that headteachers, whose experience of education and management is
assumed to be considerable, should have even less need for training.

There are opposing views. Headteacher appraisal is very different,
in many respects, from teacher appraisal. It deals with the management of the whole organization rather than a focused area of classroom teaching. It involves the head in policy-making and
implementation in several broad Areas: teaching, learning and the
curriculum, staffing, resourcing and external relations. This is a complex mix of responsibilities and the possibility of a careful appraisal
that might lead to improvement in any, or all, of these Areas is an
opportunity for the head to review his or her role and performance
within it that must be taken seriously. For heads to gain maximum
benefit from this opportunity they should receive some training in
several of the content areas mentioned above, especially the system to
be adopted, purposes of appraisal, collecting information and target
setting.

Furthermore, if heads' training can be combined with that of the
appraisers it will ensure that the parties to the process share a common
understanding of the issues involved. Combined training could also
help to reduce the unit cost of the programme by increasing the numbers taking part.

Balance between information and practice

There is a great deal of information regarding appraisal that can and
should be known and understood by participants if the scheme is to

work effectively. The main content areas and how they might be covered as part of the training are considered in detail shortly. But alongside such information there is a need for a number of practical skills, particularly relating to research methods, interviewing and report writing. Whereas the elements of these can be discussed and, to some extent, practised within workshop conditions there is also a need to consolidate them through experience gained in real situations.

Training, therefore, ideally should have built into it the possibility of monitored experience incorporating real appraisal interviews followed by feedback and discussion on the outcomes. To achieve this, it is helpful if appraisers, including any LEA officers who may be part of the scheme, are trained together. When each person has been involved as appraiser and appraisee in one or more interviews a follow-up meeting should be arranged to evaluate the outcomes, consider what problems arose and discuss how they were, or might be, overcome.

Time and costs

The amount of time necessary for appraisal training will be influenced by the factors referred to above: the needs of the participants, the content to be covered and the balance between information input and practice. These will vary between LEAs according to the amount of previous experience and training acquired by those taking part. A further determining factor may also be the LEA's INSET budget, especially the amount received for appraisal training from the Government.

For the present discussion it is only possible to suggest some guidelines based upon training schemes already provided by a few authorities. In general there is a preference for a two-day workshop, often followed by a further day to evaluate the outcomes and problems encountered in the appraisals undertaken in the intervening period.

The costs of such training will vary, depending upon:

- the venue (lower cost if using LEA's own professional centre);
- whether residential or not (residential programmes allow more time for formal and informal discussion and help to build social cohesion but are more expensive);
- travel costs (clearly depend upon where the training takes place);
- trainers' costs (can cost up to £500 a day if bought in; otherwise there is the opportunity cost of the LEA's own staff to be accounted for);
- the need for cover for those attending (during school time a teaching head will normally require cover at about £70–£90 per day);

- the size of the group (unit costs will tend to diminish as group size increases since trainer costs and some overheads can be spread over more people).

A two-day, non-residential workshop during school hours plus a one-day follow-up feedback session for twenty participants would cost about £7,000 or £350 per person. This assumes cover for three days, one external trainer and accommodation in an LEA centre. It does not take into account the time of LEA officers who may assist in the training.

The provision of training

In order to provide a working model, it will be assumed that the 'two plus one' day, non-residential format costed above will be used for a group of about twenty heads, all of whom will at some time in the future become appraisers and/or appraisees. It is also assumed that they are familiar with the skills of interviewing, having had experience of appraising their own staff. The two days will allow for eight sessions covering the six content areas as follows.

A workshop programme

The programme for a two-day workshop might be structured as in Figure 7.1.

Workshop sessions

The content areas are now considered in more detail and some suggestions as to how each session might be organized are made.

(a) The system to be adopted
Until 1991, appraisal had been voluntary and largely experimental. The six LEAs undertaking pilot projects in the national scheme all tried different approaches, all were evaluated and all reported to a national steering committee which, in turn, reported to the DES (NSG, 1989). Two Secretaries of State responded to this report (DES, 1990a, b) and, apart from certain differences (see Chapter 6, p. 62), the general approach that LEAs and schools will be expected to adopt under a compulsory scheme has become apparent.

There are now guidelines offering a clear sense of direction but they still leave some flexibility for LEAs to meet local preferences and needs. From the NSG report and the DES responses it is possible for trainers to extract and put together a number of working papers that

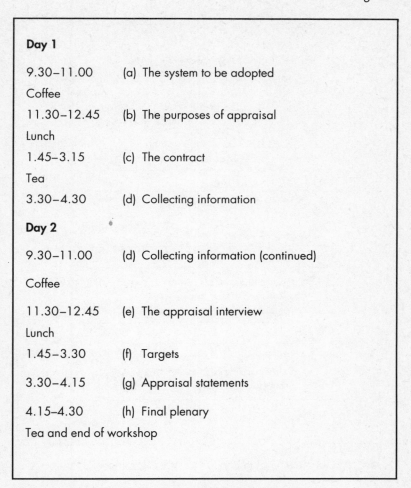

Day 1

9.30–11.00	(a)	The system to be adopted
Coffee		
11.30–12.45	(b)	The purposes of appraisal
Lunch		
1.45–3.15	(c)	The contract
Tea		
3.30–4.30	(d)	Collecting information

Day 2

9.30–11.00	(d)	Collecting information (continued)
Coffee		
11.30–12.45	(e)	The appraisal interview
Lunch		
1.45–3.30	(f)	Targets
3.30–4.15	(g)	Appraisal statements
4.15–4.30	(h)	Final plenary
Tea and end of workshop		

Figure 7.1 An appraisal training workshop timetable.

cover national recommendations regarding the selection and role of appraisers and the components of a biennial cycle of appraisal, including: the initial meeting; self-appraisal; task and/or classroom observation; collection of information; the appraisal interview; the appraisal statement; the follow-up procedures. These components can be shown diagrammatically, indicating the sequence of events and the time span over which they are spread (Figure 7.2).

Extracts from the NSG guidelines and DES regulations can be used both to explain the nature of the proposed system and to discuss the

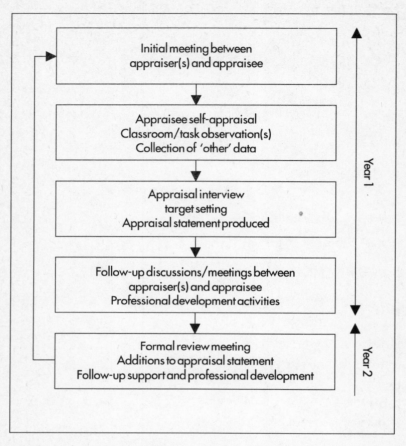

Figure 7.2   Components of the appraisal process: a biennial cycle.
Source: NSG (1989)

ramifications of applying the recommendations to the LEA scheme. The purpose will be to explain the components and structure of the scheme and to identify issues for discussion during later sessions.

(b) Purposes of appraisal
Heads and advisers about to take part in appraisal, whether as appraisers or appraisees, should be familiar with the underlying approach and the general philosophy adopted by the LEA. These will to some extent be determined by national guidelines but also by the nature of local needs and circumstances. There are political agendas

involved in determining the nature of appraisal. There are pressures towards accountability, the use of performance indicators, links with disciplinary procedures and payment by results. There are counter pressures suggesting that appraisal should be solely concerned with development – both of the management of the school and of the head (see Chapters 1 and 2). Those involved in appraisal need to be aware of these pressures, where they come from and what authority they have, and of what approach appraisers and appraisees might be expected to adopt.

A structured exercise used in teacher appraisal training (Hewton, 1988b) can be adapted for headteachers. This requires groups, usually of about six to eight participants, to discuss and then place in priority order a series of statements (written on cards) regarding the purposes of headteacher appraisal. Statements can be discarded by the group and there are blank cards on which additional statements can be written. The cards given to each group contain the following statements:

To review the aims, plans and policies of the school.
To reward good headteachers.
To provide feedback on performance.
To review management style.
To clarify career goals.
To demonstrate the existence of accountability.
To ensure that the school is complying with the demands of the national curriculum.
To tackle problems presented by weak heads.
To reduce the sense of isolation that some heads feel.
To help heads meet the challenge of greater autonomy for schools.
To assess heads' developmental needs.
To clarify and explore the head's vision for the school.
To improve the learning opportunities of pupils.
To provide support and encouragement.
To improve the management of the school.
To set targets for the future development of the school.
To clarify career goals.

These seventeen statements are not comprehensive but they are sufficiently diverse to require the groups to discuss many of the key issues associated with the purposes of appraisal, such as: accountability versus development; school improvement versus career development; links with reward or discipline; the need for support and feedback on performance; the underlying aim of improving pupil learning.

Normally sub-groups will need an hour to carry out the task of choosing the most important purposes and then a further half-hour to share their ideas in plenary. Participants can then be reminded that they will be required to agree the purposes of the appraisal in the 'contract' which they will enter into with their appraiser or appraisee (see Chapter 4). They can be asked if they would accept the general statement: 'the main aim of appraisal should be to improve the functioning of the school as it affects services provided for pupils and staff.' If this statement is accepted, then the other purposes agreed as important in the structured exercise above can be seen as contributing towards this general aim.

(c) The contract

The contract is intended to make explicit the purposes of the appraisal about to be undertaken and the way in which it will be conducted. The nature of the contract is discussed in detail in Chapter 4. For the purposes of the workshop the participants need to be made aware of the Areas of headship, the possible Aspects associated with each and the way in which agreement might be reached concerning the choice of Areas and Aspects for review.

For this purpose it is suggested that Figure 4.1 (p. 45) is used as the basis for discussion. Participants might then be set the following task.

> In pairs, discuss with your partner which would be, for you, the most important Area to review in your first appraisal. Try to justify your choice. What Aspects of this Area would you consider to be the most important for you and your appraiser(s) to concentrate upon in a real interview?
>
> Take fifteen minutes each on this task and write down for your own future use the Area and Aspects chosen.

A further fifteen minutes should then be allowed in plenary for issues and problems to be discussed.

(d) Collecting information

This session follows on from the previous one and requires participants to consider ways in which information might be collected in connection with the Areas and Aspects of role agreed in the first part of the initial meeting. In Chapter 6 the sources of information for appraisal were discussed under the following headings: the appraiser's own knowledge, documents, observed situations, formal and informal interviews, and questionnaires.

In connection with the first of these (the appraisee's own knowledge) it is useful to concentrate upon the self-evaluation form that is proposed for use in the scheme. One way of doing this is to send the form to participants beforehand and ask them to complete it for the workshop as though they were about to engage in a real appraisal. The session can then begin with a consideration of the usefulness of the form and whether it could be improved in any way. It is helpful to allow an exchange of views in pairs before a plenary discussion.

The remainder of the session can then be devoted to other means of collecting information. Given the relatively short time available, the organizers should explain to participants the various possible sources of information and then discuss with them the methods and problems of tapping such sources. More detail can be added in the first session of the following day.

The second session requires participants to consider how they might plan a visit to a school in order to collect information in the following hypothetical circumstances.

The head of a group 5 primary school has agreed with the appraiser (an experienced head of a similar school) that the appraisal will focus upon two Areas:

A Management of the curriculum with particular reference to monitoring the curriculum in action; the implementation of a policy for teaching and learning and the quality of written work in years 4 and 5.
B External relations, with particular reference to parent–teacher consultation and report writing.

In relation to A it was agreed that the appraiser would:

(a) sit in on sessions in which the head meets individual teachers to discuss samples of pupils' work;
(b) shadow the head while he or she is involved in classroom observation for the purpose of monitoring the implementation of the policy for teaching and learning. The particular aspect of policy to be monitored will be the organization of cooperative group work.

In relation to B it was agreed that the appraiser should read the appropriate documentation and then talk with members of staff to gain their perceptions on current forms of parent–teacher consultation.

Task (in groups of three)
Put yourself in the situation of the appraiser and, as a group, plan in writing a day visit to the school in order to carry out all of the tasks necessary to collect the information referred to above.

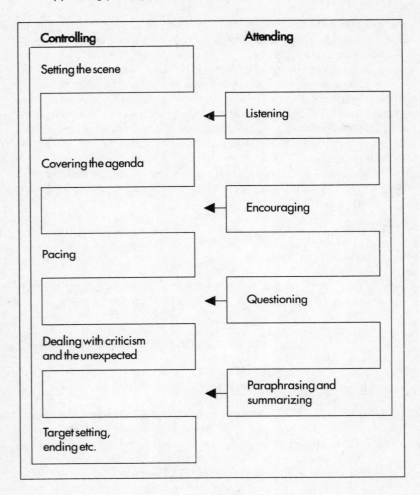

Figure 7.3 The complementary skills of interviewing.

If documents have already been produced by the LEA to help appraisers and appraisees draw up the contract, especially with regard to collecting information, then such form(s) might be used in this task. A possible form of this kind is shown in Appendix 4.

About an hour should be allowed for the exercise and the remainder of the session will then be devoted to discussion of the problems which could arise and how they might be overcome.

(e) The interview

The main purpose of this session is to review (there will be no time to practise) the skills of interviewing and to consider how the interview might be structured.

The idea that there are two interlocking sets of skills – attending and controlling – can be illustrated by means of a diagram, as in Figure 7.3. The two sets of skills should be discussed, especially the possible tensions between 'attending', which requires the appraiser to listen while maintaining a low profile, and 'controlling', which is akin to chairing a meeting and working through an agenda on time.

There are various formats for structuring an interview and these are suggested in Chapter 6 (pp. 66–7). These could be put to participants as possible agendas and views sought as to which they would find most appropriate. It has been assumed here that the heads concerned have already had some training and experience in interviewing. If this is not the case a different programme is necessary (see below).

(f) Targets and appraisal statements

Heads may, from time to time, use targets as part of their work but generally these are not set out in the kind of detail appropriate for appraisal. For this reason some input from the trainers concerning the

---

S pecific   (rather than general)

M anageable   (feasible within the constraints)

A ppropriate   (for the head at that time)

R elevant   (to the needs identified)

T imed   (clear stage or completion dates)

I nformative   (contains sufficient information to avoid any ambiguity)

E valuation relating to

S uccess criteria   (specifying ways in which it is possible to verify that the target has been achieved)

Figure 7.4   The elements of an appraisal target.

Writing targets

During the appraisal interview you have made notes of some of the statements made by the appraisee that indicate possible target areas for discussion.

'I must make more time for policy-making and planning.'

'Teacher–parent communication is something of a problem.'

'We are spending much too much time on unproductive meetings and staff regard them as a waste of time.'

'I need to get to grips with the new computer system for budgeting.'

'I'm sure I could give more responsibility to my deputy.'

'I ought to get round to producing a staff development policy.'

'I must start preparing staff for appraisal.'

'I'm not at all satisfied with the way we have introduced the new science curriculum.'

One person agrees to accept one of these statements as though it applied to him or her and work with the group to turn it into a statement that complies with the SMARTIES criteria. If none of the above seems applicable please invent one.

Figure 7.5 Training task: writing targets.

nature of targets is necessary along with the opportunity for participants to write one or two.

Chapter 6 (pp. 72–5) deals with some of the concepts and issues associated with targets and these might be referred to in a training session. A summary of the key elements of a target, however, is contained within the acronym SMARTIES, and Figure 7.4 might be useful as an aid to discussion. Discussion of the elements in Figure

7.4 normally takes about twenty minutes and an hour can then be devoted to writing a target in groups of four. The set task is shown in Figure 7.5.

It might be suggested that each group writes out its target on flip-chart paper and exhibits it for others to see. This also gives the organizers a chance to comment and to reinforce the key elements of a target.

At the beginning of the next session there should be time to discuss any issues of concern relating to the nature of statements, who writes them, their content, who has access to them, where they will be kept and their 'shelf life'. National guidelines referred to in the first session may be reconsidered. The discussion is often lengthy on this topic and time should be allowed for anxieties to surface and be fully and openly considered. Organizers might like to refer again to the section of Chapter 6 (pp. 76–80) dealing with this matter.

Heads are often reassured if they see what an appraisal statement might look like and the kind of language that is appropriate in such documents. The example statement in Chapter 6 (p. 78) could be used for discussion purposes.

The day might end with a reminder of how appraisers will be allocated to appraisees, ways in which heads might object to the choice, documents to be used, critical dates etc. By the time they leave, participants should know what will happen next, what steps are necessary to complete their first appraisal and the date of the follow-up day.

The follow-up day

The follow-up day will generally follow the workshop after two or three months during which the heads involved will have had time to engage in the appraisal of other heads. The aims of the day will be to:

- share experiences among those taking part in the appraisal scheme;
- deal with problems as they arise;
- provide feedback to the LEA concerning the workshops and outcomes of the scheme;
- suggest ways in which documents, procedures or support might be improved.

With these aims in mind the programme for the day might be structured as in Figure 7.6. It is important that the LEA representatives take part in the discussions, take note of matters that require change and act upon the agreed recommendations.

9.30–10.30　Two pairs (appraiser and appraisee) to present to the group their experiences

Coffee

11.00–12.30　In groups of six, continue from first session by sharing experiences as both appraiser and appraisee and identify key issues relating to the process and the materials in use.

Lunch

2.00–3.15　In plenary identify the most important issues.

Tea

3.30–4.15　Decide recommendations for improving the system

Figure 7.6　A timetable for the appraisal training follow-up day.

Longer programmes

The programme outlined above takes account of the fact that training is expensive and that INSET budgets, even if increased by special grants for appraisal, have to stretch to cover many demands. It is fairly comprehensive provided organizers are satisfied that those concerned have adequate information-collecting and interviewing skills. If this is not the case then training may well require either a residential workshop that will provide extra sessions or a three-day initial workshop.

In a longer workshop it will be possible to build in one or preferably two sessions covering the particular skills necessary for:

- interviewing for information (e.g. staff, parents, pupils, governors);
- observation (of any task that the head may be engaged in – classroom observation may require special attention in itself);
- document analysis (especially of the kind of documents that would repay analysis and contain the type of information that may be sought);
- questionnaire construction (where it is felt that responses from a larger group than can be obtained by interviewing are required).

It will also be possible to build in interview practice, and this can be done by requiring all heads to complete a self-review form before the workshop. Volunteers are then interviewed by three other participants, who use the self-review form as their main source of information. Each interviewer deals with about one-third of the agenda. An appraisal statement, together with targets, is prepared at the end of the interview. This process requires a separate room for each group of four and, allowing for preparation and feedback time, will normally take a whole morning or afternoon. Full details of the method are explained in *The Appraisal Interview* (Hewton, 1988).

Summary

In this chapter issues concerning training for headteacher appraisal were addressed and possible ways of organizing such training were suggested. The main issues relate to: possible content to be covered; identifying the training needs of appraisers and appraisees; obtaining an appropriate balance between the provision of information and practice; and time needed for training, including the costs involved.

A programme over three days involving a two-day workshop plus a follow-up day for review was suggested. Content coverage included discussion of: the system of appraisal to be adopted; the purposes of appraisal for headteachers; agreeing a contract between appraisers and appraisee; collecting information; the interview; targets and appraisal statements.

It was suggested that a longer workshop, involving about an extra day, would be needed to allow time for (a) more detailed coverage of research skills for collecting information and (b) practice appraisal interviews.

8

Appraisal in action

In this chapter we move from the elements of a model, its possibilities and problems and the nature of the training that should accompany its use, to the experiences of two heads in one LEA where the model has recently been introduced. Roy Grigg and Robin Barnett, both heads of medium to large primary schools, agreed to keep a record of their appraisal experiences, the former as appraiser and the latter as appraisee. Their reports form the basis of this chapter.

The LEA concerned has a history of involvement in staff development and all schools are required to produce and implement a whole-school staff development policy, of which an essential part is an annual review for each member of staff. All heads (and often other staff in the school) receive training covering staff development policies and the skills of interviewing required for the annual review.

It was not long before many headteachers realized the importance and value of the scheme for their staff and began to see the possible benefits of a review system for themselves. Small-scale experiments began, mainly instigated by colleague heads in neighbouring schools, and as a result a body of experience was created that was later tapped by the LEA in response to national initiatives. It set up a small group with a view to drawing up a voluntary, county-wide scheme for heads. This group comprised six heads with some experience of staff development review in general and head-teacher review in particular. The authors of this book acted as consultants to the group and many of the elements of the system that emerged are incorporated in the model described in earlier chapters.

Originally, the title 'Head Teacher Development Review' was adopted by the group because 'review' was a term familiar and widely accepted in the authority and also because 'development' emphasized the particular aim and thrust of the scheme. However, since that time *appraisal* has become a mandatory activity for all schools and for the remainder of this chapter the term 'appraisal' will be used.

The two heads who shared in the writing of this chapter both had early experience of appraisal in the county, were volunteers for the new county-wide scheme and took part in the training programme in 1990. Over the period of a year each will appraise two other heads and will be appraised themselves. The LEA allocates the appraisers but appraisees have the option to refuse and to ask for an alternative person. The authority attempts to match pairs according to the type of school and the past experience of the heads concerned. Since the scheme has been in operation the negative option has rarely, if at all, been used.

The reports from the two heads are structured as follows: background; preparation and early contact; the initial meeting and contract; information gathering; the appraisal interview; the appraisal statement and targets; reflections. The appraiser's perspective is presented first, followed by the appraiser's experience. The chapter ends with some conclusions linking both sets of comments to issues raised earlier in the book. Reference to, or examples of, some of the materials used in the scheme are appended.

The appraiser's experience

Background

I worked in schools in three authorities before joining my present employer in 1968. Since then I have worked in five schools, including a small village school, an infants school and a large urban primary. The bulk of this time has been at my present school, in a growing country town. I became the head when it opened in 1974.

I became involved in review/appraisal work in 1985 as part of a pilot project on staff development. This gave me some experience as an appraiser of both teaching and non-teaching staff. I was also appraised on two occasions by two staff colleagues working with a senior primary adviser and on two further occasions by an adviser working alone. I was a member of an early working party on headteacher appraisal in 1987 and, more recently, a task group set up by the county in January

1990, which led to the current headteacher appraisal initiative. I joined the first group of volunteers as both an appraiser and an appraisee and attended the initial training sessions provided by the LEA. This group set the pattern for the three training sessions which followed and thorough which materials were developed and 'fine tuned' before being used in actual appraisals.

I welcomed the wider development of appraisal, believing that it is essential for headteachers to be fully involved in a process that they expect teachers in their schools to accept as a matter of routine. My earlier experiences helped me to prepare for the appraisal of a colleague and although I felt confident about the task ahead, I was also anxious that I should not fail to conduct an acceptable professional appraisal, meeting all the challenges it might bring. I knew that only thorough preparation on my part could help to ensure this.

I decided to keep a journal to record information, thoughts, feelings, reactions and comments alongside specific appraisal notes.

Preparation and early contact

The allocation of appraisers to appraisees by a County Hall official was completed in July 1990 and I was assigned to appraise the experienced head of a large junior school situated about 30 miles from my own. I had known him for some years and we had previously worked together on a county-wide school-focused staff development scheme.

Early contact by telephone (July 1990) enabled us to agree a date for our initial meeting at his school in September and possible dates for the appraisal interview in November. One of these dates was later confirmed with the general primary adviser who would attend the main interview.

I received the materials we would need from County Hall in early September 1990. The pack contained guidance on the agreed process of appraisal and documents to be sent to the appraisee to help him prepare for the initial meeting. These were posted to him about two weeks in advance of the meeting.

The initial meeting and contract

The school, built in the 1950s, seemed large compared with my own and I found the size and resource space impressive. My appraisee had made all staff fully aware of the purpose of my visit and I was introduced to several of them during the morning. He had planned my programme to include a tour of the school, a visit to the staffroom and time for our own discussions in his office. He had also completed the self-review form which I had forwarded to him. We talked through the notes he had written to help his own reflections and he expanded on his view of the current situation at the school. We then considered, in turn, the various Areas of headship that might be covered in the appraisal.

We agreed to focus upon the management and development of finance/resources and external relations but in practice these shaded over into other Areas, particularly when we discussed his own professional development. Our preliminary discussions were detailed and at one stage could easily have turned into a full appraisal discussion.

We then concentrated upon the particular Aspects of the agreed Areas and decided what information it would be necessary to collect, the people I should meet to obtain it and the documentation I would need to read. Two half-day visits were arranged for this and we produced a preliminary timetable. The dates in October were some way ahead but were the earliest we could manage.

Final arrangements for the visits were confirmed by telephone and I later received details in writing (see Example Document 1, at the end of this chapter).

Information gathering

I felt that careful planning for this aspect of the appraisal was very important because questioning staff about the role of their head-teacher needed a sensitive approach. We had arranged that I should speak to seven people – five staff, a parent and the chair of governors – and I decided that a uniform approach at the outset of each interview was important. To achieve this I wrote a brief introductory statement which I used as an *aide-mémoire* for my opening comments at each interview (see Example Document 2 at the end of this chapter). I also prepared a prompt list for myself, setting out questions pertinent to the chosen Areas for appraisal. Additional questions arose naturally out of the discussions.

A room was set aside for my use so that interviews would be uninterrupted. Those involved were cooperative and responded in an open, positive way to the process, and I was pleased to hear later that they had found the interviews interesting and valuable. On the first visit I saw four people, including the chair of governors, and interviews generally took between 30 and 60 minutes.

Three more interviews were completed during the second visit and I allowed some time to study the documentation I had requested on my previous visit (see Example Document 3). The final interview with a member of staff took place shortly after lunch. I then felt that I had gathered enough information to enable me to approach the actual appraisal interview with confidence. This was scheduled for 15 November, leaving a gap of five weeks (including a half-term break) for reflection and preparation. This was longer than we would have wished but was unavoidable because of the need to coordinate dates between three people: appraiser, appraisee and adviser. The gap did not, however, seem to detract in any way from the appraisal process.

I kept my journal up-to-date after each visit and included general observations about what I had seen and the people I had met so that I built up as full a picture as possible of the role of the headteacher and the school. My final preparations for the appraisal interview were made a few days beforehand so that matters would be fresh in my mind. My journal and notes from the three visits were invaluable and from these I prepared a prompt list that gave me confidence and helped to ensure that the interview had an edge and a purpose. Letters confirming the interview were sent to the appraisee and adviser giving details of the scope of the appraisal.

Note: This appraisal took place before the Secretary of State announced his intention of making appraisal compulsory. At this stage the LEA were operating a voluntary scheme in which the parties to the appraisal process could decide for themselves exactly what information to collect and what methods to use. Observation of classroom teaching or other task performance was not then mandatory. In the future it will be.

The appraisal interview

The interview was held in the head's room on 15 November using three comfortable chairs around a low table. Over coffee, we agreed what the adviser's role should be and expressed the intention that the interview would take the form of a discussion involving all three participants. It was also agreed that I should be responsible for writing the first draft of the appraisal statement.

In my introduction I referred to what had been agreed at the initial meeting, thus setting the scene for the discussions and at the same time providing the adviser with useful background information.

We talked for over an hour before taking a break in the staff room. This came at the right time, giving us an opportunity to mull over what had been said and to gather our thoughts. It was interesting to note that teachers in the room were anxious for the head and keen to know that his 'ordeal' was going well.

The session continued for another hour or so and involved reflection, more detailed analysis of points raised earlier and discussions about possible targets. We arranged to meet again on 22 November to discuss and agree the draft appraisal statement, which I would prepare and send to the head beforehand.

The appraisal statement and targets

The notes I had used at the appraisal interview, together with comments added throughout this session, formed the basis for the appraisal statement. Despite having this material as a guide it took me some time to complete the document. The need to choose words with care, making all the points as concisely as possible, was always in my mind. My word processor proved helpful in completing this task. The resulting document was a little over two sides of A4 (typewritten) paper, and concluded with a separate section on targets. (These are referred to by the appraisee later.)

I approached the meeting to discuss the draft with some apprehension, uncertain as to how it might have been received. We read it aloud together and made a few comments but in the end it was accepted as it stood. We signed three copies, one for each of us, and a third for the general primary adviser who was not present at this meeting.

Reflections

Appraisal is intended principally to benefit the appraisee and ultimately the school and its pupils but I found that I had gained a great deal from it myself. It was a rewarding experience during which I learned much about approaching others on, sometimes, delicate issues. I was pleased that my appraisee seemed well satisfied and ready to take some positive action associated with agreed targets.

This appraisal was conducted by two headteachers who had volunteered to take part in the county scheme. There was, therefore, a full commitment to the process that may not always exist in a compulsory system. To overcome this problem trust and confidence will have to be built up through careful training and participation in planning by those involved.

A peer group approach has the advantage that those involved are in touch with the issues of the day and this, from my experience of appraisal, is an important element. Some may think that peer appraisal, on the lines described above, is a 'soft option' and clearly circumstances could arise when this might prove to be the case. An LEA scheme must, therefore, be organized to prevent this from happening. The involvement of advisers at appraisal interviews is one way of helping to achieve this and it also provides a general monitoring process for the authority, which is important in maintaining standards and consistency.

The fact that this is not a 'top-down' system does, I feel, put pressure on the appraiser, who holds the prime responsibility for the direction of the appraisal process. On occasions it felt like walking on egg shells and much depends on the professionalism of the participants and the match of appraiser to appraisee at the outset. The appraisee must clearly have respect for the appraiser. The option for the appraisee to reject the allocated appraiser (before the appraiser is given notice of the allocation) helps to achieve this goal.

Good appraisal work can best be achieved when sufficient time for the process is available. A peer approach requires that headteachers, and often other staff who need to be interviewed, must take time away from their other duties. There is thus a price to be paid by the schools involved in an appraisal. If, overall, the appraisal process is successful, this is time well spent and will, in the long run, repay the schools through improved performance and positive professional development.

My journal indicated that I spent 31 hours (including eight hours travelling) on the appraisal. This is far more than the three (probably to become only two in the future) days' cover allowed by the LEA. Perhaps the process can be trimmed as people become more experienced but I can foresee problems for heads of small schools who might find it difficult, or impossible, to leave their classrooms or schools for any length of time. Resourcing is, therefore, a matter that will need careful consideration.

The appraisal pack of materials proved most useful to both the appraiser and appraisee. It assisted in maintaining smooth progress as the appraisal proceeded, helped in arranging the contract and ensured that adequate preparation was made for the initial and main appraisal interviews.

The confidentiality and circulation of the appraisal statement remains a matter of some concern, especially if the adviser's copies are stored in a central place – say on file at County Hall where unauthorized staff might have access to them. National guidelines might, in the end, solve this problem but it needs to be carefully considered when local schemes are established.

Appraisers will normally make notes throughout the appraisal process and some, as in my case, record information on a word processor. Confidentiality and all aspects of the Data Protection Act must be fully respected and files erased and notes destroyed once appraisal work has been completed. Appraisers who do not type or have access to word processors may have to write reports in longhand since school secretaries should, normally, not be involved.

The second phase of this appraisal will take place in a year's time and will look at the progress made on the targets set. I would speculate that the majority will have been achieved and that some will have been extended and developed further than originally envisaged.

Although experiencing some anxiety throughout, I very much enjoyed the process. It requires a full, professional commitment to be truly successful and can provide as many benefits for the appraiser as it does for the appraisee and the school.

The appraisee's experience

Background

My first appointment as head was to a newly opened primary school in the south, where during my years in post I introduced an informal appraisal interview scheme for all teachers. In 1981 I moved to my present post as head of a large junior school with over twenty teachers and 500 children, and again I introduced a similar scheme. This may have been a factor contributing to the school's involvement in the county's staff development pilot project in 1985. In 1986 the local primary adviser responded to my request to appraise my work as head. In 1989 I took part, with another local head, in an experiment whereby paired heads took on the roles of appraiser and appraisee for each other.

These experiences, which I had initiated and welcomed, laid the foundations for the more formal and structured head appraisal scheme that has now been introduced and for which, once again, I volunteered. The fact that my involvement in the appraisal was on a voluntary basis meant that I wished to be appraised. This may not necessarily be so when the scheme is introduced on a compulsory basis and it could well be daunting for heads who have not had the advantage of previous appraisal experience.

The present scheme was introduced in a two-day workshop that did much to allay any initial uncertainties I may have had. Nevertheless, the detail and complexity of the more formal system seemed awesome, especially given the already heavy work-load felt by most heads at the present time.

I accepted my appraiser, the head of another primary school, having had the right to reject him. I knew him to be a person of integrity and had worked with him some years earlier in helping to introduce staff development policies into county primary schools. I therefore had confidence and trust in him – a vital factor in this exercise.

Preparation and early contact

I received from my appraiser a package of materials provided by the county containing detailed instructions, a self-evaluation pro forma, prompt lists etc., and I found these to be invaluable in planning and preparing for my review. Considerable heart-searching took place during completion of the self-review form but this was a definite aid in helping to clatify my thoughts about which Areas of headship should be selected.

At this stage I had mixed feelings about my work, ranging from a sense of being relatively successful in all areas to feeling inadequate in most. The need to put forward suggestions for two Areas to be appraised made me wonder whether I would be suggesting to my appraiser that I was faultless in the remaining areas. And the two Areas that I might like to nominate might not coincide with those that my staff would have chosen had they been asked. Knowing that they were to be asked to comment on my performance as a manager and facilitator in these Areas also made me slightly anxious.

I did not feel that it would be particularly useful to consider 'management of the curriculum' because of the considerable progress made by school working parties set up over a year ago. Nor did I want to spend much time on 'management of staff', because our ongoing, school staff development programme had recently received a great deal of attention and seemed to be working well. But would the staff necessarily agree with my reasons for not putting forward these areas?

The initial meeting and contract

The perhaps unnecessary doubts about my priorities were alleviated during my initial meeting with the appraiser. Merely talking through how I had arrived at my preferred Areas for appraisal helped to clarify my thoughts and reassure me that I had chosen well. Although he could have exercised the right to challenge my choice there was no hint during discussions that this would be necessary.

The Areas chosen by me and agreed by my appraiser were 'management of finance and resources' and 'management of external relations'. In both of these Areas I considered myself to be reasonably efficient but knew that there was more that could be done. The budget management aspect of the job was a departure from my previous experiences and I was also aware that there was a need to improve communications, especially outside the school.

The third Area, my own professional development, was an uncertain element in the appraisal, especially as I do not envisage a career beyond my present school. But, as will be seen later, ideas about my own management style and priorities, which emerged during discussions on the other two Areas, led me to consider a target of a kind I had not anticipated. This made me realize that professional development is not just about 'onward and upward' career progress but also about my own development as a person and a manager in my current post.

Information gathering

I informed the staff about the appraisal process and was able to suggest people who could assist my reviewer in gathering information. We identified two deputy heads because of their knowledge of the management of the school, their regular contact with me and their experience of my management style. It was also suggested that two teachers should assist the appraiser. One had been at the school for 17 years and had worked with my predecessor; the other had joined the school as a probationer a year ago.

The chair of governors, a parent who helps regularly in school and the school secretary were identified as further sources of information. All willingly consented to take part in the exercise. I asked them to speak frankly and explained that it was the genuine intent to assist in my development as a manager and that this would ultimately benefit the school. In addition, the appraiser asked to see various documents relevant to the Areas to be investigated. I was relieved to find that all of these were available and up-to-date!

After their interviews the deputies, the teachers, the secretary and the chair of governors all told me how they had enjoyed the discussion and found it useful and stimulating. The fact that they all spoke to me about this acted as a morale booster for both myself and, I understand, the appraiser. All those interviewed mentioned that they appreciated the fact that their opinion was valued.

The appraisal interview

Because of pressure of work there was a two-month gap between the initial meeting and the main interview, which was longer than recommended by the county. This meant that I had ample time for reflection about the two agreed Areas. Indeed the initial meeting was so interesting and constructive that we inadvertently began to cover some of the questions to be addressed at the main interview. We had consciously to hold back from going into issues in too much depth. However, ideas were triggered in my mind and these evolved further during the intervening weeks. This meant, in practice, that developments were already taking place as the appraisal proceeded.

The interview lasted for about three hours with a short break in the middle. The local primary adviser joined us at the meeting and it was made clear from the outset that it would be a structured three-sided discussion – which it turned out to be.

The appraiser had prepared the ground for discussion extremely well and by the skilful use of directed, but open-ended, questions was able to encourage me to talk in detail about the selected Areas of management. I was surprised to find how quickly the three hours passed but in that time all agenda items were covered and targets were set.

The interview enabled me to explore the ideas that had begun to consolidate in my mind as the result of reflection, discussion and some background reading I had done following the initial meeting. In addition, during discussions about my own professional development, an issue emerged which I had not previously considered. This related to the use of my own time. I had, during the interview, made a statement to the effect that I was not satisfied that I was doing all I should in monitoring the implementation of the National Curriculum in the classroom. It was interesting that we should have come to this issue through discussions about my own use of time rather than from a specific consideration of the Area 'management and development of the curriculum', which was not on our agenda. This illustrates how difficult it would be, even if this was the intention, to isolate entirely the different Areas of the job.

The discussion led me to consider the possibility of delegating to one of the two deputy heads a mainly non-teaching timetable so that he might take on some of the work. This would release me to visit classrooms to ascertain how the National Curriculum was being delivered. It would also enable me to share more management decisions with the deputy, which would be an advantage to both of us. It would, however, be a considerable departure from the existing practice, whereby both deputies teach almost full-time, and would mean reducing the time spent by one deputy in the special needs department.

During the interview I was pleased to discuss this possibility but I realized it would need much thought and discussion with the staff before any action could be taken. Nevertheless, the idea caused me to rethink the way in which senior staff are deployed at the school. The advantage of having an experienced fellow head who can stand back and discuss such ideas objectively is possibly one of the main strengths of the appraisal process.

The adviser's presence was also helpful as she was able to expand on comments made by the appraiser and myself. I believe the adviser's role would be even more crucial in a situation where the appraiser and appraisee were less experienced or where a pressing need for immediate change was identified.

On two or three occasions during the interview the appraiser was able to comment favourably and positively on how the staff viewed my leadership style and this feedback was reassuring and much appreciated.

The appraisal statement and targets

A further meeting took place a week after the interview when the appraiser presented the draft report, which I was happy to accept as it stood. It contained a number of targets, some of which related to the two Areas chosen for review and some concerning matters that had arisen from general discussions about internal management issues and my own professional development. The targets related to the following actions:

1 Developing a budgeting system for class teachers.
2 Carrying out a review of expenditure procedures.
3 Improving communications with parents, especially regarding the curriculum.
4 Preparing a regular whole-school newsletter.
5 Using management meetings to share forward thinking with colleagues.
6 Improving communication procedures within the school.
7 Reviewing the allocation of work between myself and the deputies generally but with the particular aim of allowing me to monitor the curriculum in action.

By the time the appraisal statement was written and agreed I had already taken action with regard to five of the above targets.

Target 7, relating to the use of my time and that of my deputies, is an interesting one and an ongoing challenge. The action plan associated with it requires me to meet the deputies for a detailed discussion this term and to ascertain their views. I will have to convince them of the value of the exercise but a good case can be made by stressing the importance of having a skilled practitioner available to monitor the curriculum and advise colleagues in the classroom. There are also advantages for the deputy who will be asked to take on some of my current administrative work. His own learning in this respect will be helpful when he applies for promotion.

Assuming that one of the deputies agrees to the proposal it will be necessary to re-negotiate his job description. The experiment might begin on a small scale and then expand if it proves successful. It would also be necessary to explain the plan to other members of staff and to coordinate any changes with a new timetable for the year commencing September 1991. The detailed action plan for this particular and potentailly far-reaching target is therefore emerging.

Reflections

The fact that my appraiser was the head of a reasonably large school was important. I do not believe the head of a very small school would necessarily have had the same insight. Careful matching of appraiser and appraisee is therefore important.

No major problems were encountered during the appraisal and this was, at least partly, because the appraiser and I had already experienced similar procedures. This enabled us to prepare the ground thoroughly and to anticipate any potential problems, such as the selection of people to be interviewed and their adequate preparation for the task. Keeping the staff fully informed was a vital element in the process.

We were participating in an experimental scheme in which we had agreed to act as both appraiser and appraisee, although not to each other, during a three-month period. This added considerably to an already heavy work-load and I would not recommend that any head be asked to undertake the two roles simultaneously.

As mentioned earlier, the review proceeded satisfactorily because of the participants' willingness to be involved and because of our mutual trust and respect. When these factors are not present already, the ground must be thoroughly prepared through good communication, training and support. However, the advantages are so great that I would recommend the procedure to every headteacher.

Some conclusions

The two sets of comments indicate a satisfactory process resulting in a number of important targets being set. There are several factors which contributed to this.

Both parties had received training in appraisal and both were able to build upon earlier positive experiences of the process.

They were satisfied with the pairing and a high degree of trust existed between the parties, which created confidence throughout.

The initial meeting proved to be important in preparing the ground. From both sets of comments it seems that this almost turned into a full interview in which some matters started to be discussed in depth. Both felt that this should be avoided since information necessary for proper analysis had yet to be obtained.

The pro forma proved a useful aid to reflection and enabled the appraisee to think through which Areas of headship he would prefer to focus upon. He was then able to justify his preference to the appraiser without difficulty.

The appraisee was able to take a leading role in suggesting who should be approached in order to obtain information. The system, however, is not meant to be one-sided. The appraiser was satisfied with the choice but asserted his own position by asking for a series of documents. The importance of preparing staff for the appraiser's visit was also highlighted.

There are several other matters that are of importance generally and that will assume even greater significance when appraisal is introduced nationally.

The interview itself was not unduly long (about three hours) and it seems that a great deal happened between the initial meeting and the main interview. This emphasizes the point that appraisal is a great deal more than just an interview and involves both the parties in a lengthy process of discussion, negotiation, planning, preparing, information gathering and report writing plus the action necessary to set out, implement and evaluate targets.

The time necessary for the appraisal of headteachers should not be underestimated and the analysis of the overall time involved in this review (approximately 50 hours for everyone concerned) is significant. Will such amounts of time be available when all heads have to be appraised within a national system?

There is concern about the part the appraisal statement should play. This is a matter that still causes anxiety given the content of Circular 12/91 (see Chapter 6). It is clear that the statement is intended to be made available to the 'chairman of the governing body' and to the Chief Education Officer and any LEA officer or adviser specifically designated by him or her. This requirement is likely to produce short reports that disclose very little apart from brief summaries of the main points covered, together with targets.

The adviser's role in the appraisal described in this chapter was restricted to the main interview, but it was acknowledged by the appraiser and appraisee to have been important and helpful. It was also indicated by the appraisee that, with less experienced heads, the adviser could have a far more important role to play.

The role of the adviser in appraisal was discussed at a follow-up meeting of heads and advisers arranged to monitor the scheme after the first round of interviews. All heads commented upon the valuable part played by advisers during their interviews and this may indicate that their initial anxieties about having an adviser present had been dispelled. The advisers welcomed the opportunity to be involved and commented upon their own learning, which had occurred as a result of taking part in the interviews.

Materials used in the review

The following documents used in this interview have already been described in other parts of the book.

Initial letter to the appraisee from the appraiser (Chapter 4).

Areas and Aspects of headship for review, 'map' and prompt list (Chapter 4).

The pro forma to be completed by the appraisee (Chapter 5 and Appendix 1).

Letter from appraisee head to staff in the school, explaining the head's appraisal process (Chapter 5).

The following pages contain some of the other documents used in the appraisal described in this chapter, particularly in the information gathering process.

Example Document 1

Confirmation of Areas and Aspects selected and programme for collecting information

Areas and Aspects

1   Management of finance/resources

   (a)   Capitation priorities
   (b)   Management of time
   (c)   Housekeeping practices

2   Management of external relations

   (a)   Parents
   (b)   Communications – internal/staff/parents/governors/
           community

3   Personal and professional development

Interviews arranged

Monday 8 October:	(D/Head) 9.45–10.40 ('B' Allowance Holder) 11.00–11.30 (Main Professional Grade Teacher) 11.35–12.05 (Ch. of Gov.) 12.10–12.40
Thursday 11 October:	(D/Head) 9.45–10.40 (Parent) 11.00–11.30 View of requested documentation (School Sec.) 1.05–2.00

Example Document 2

Appraiser's *aide-mémoire* of points to make when opening the interview

Interviewee: _____

Date: _____

The following areas have been highlighted through discussions with the head and in order to build a picture of current practice it has been agreed that I should talk with you.

Areas to be covered

Management of finance/resources

    Capitation priorities
    Management of time
    Housekeeping practices

Management of external relations

    Parents
    Communications – internal, staff, parents, governors, community

This is an open process through which I hope to learn of your viewpoint on matters related to this appraisal.

I may take notes in our discussions as an *aide-mémoire* for my future use.

Do you wish to ask any questions about the appraisal process and your involvement in it?

Are you happy with the arrangements as I have explained them?

Example Document 3

Documentation – information for appraisal

To the Head

It would be helpful to have sight/copies of the following documentation if it is available:

    Budget planning papers
    Capitation priority list 1989/90, 1990/91
    Spending control records – capitation/staff/supply teachers etc.
    Any budget information given to staff
    Any budget information given to governors
    Blue Ledger (LMS)
    Sample governors' report
    Sample letters to parents
    Sample staff memos
    Prospectus
    School brochure
    Sample staff meeting minutes
    Sample management meeting minutes
    Staff guidelines or a school policy statement
    Staff handbook
    School magazine

9
Primary headship and appraisal in the 1990s

We have described in earlier chapters a model of appraisal for primary headteachers which has shown itself to be feasible in terms of its demands on resources and its capacity to meet the purposes for which it is intended. In doing so we have construed headship as a role invested in one person, the headteacher, who in terms of his or her appointment:

> shall be the leader of the school community and shall be the principal representative of the school in its relationships with the authority that maintains it, the governing body, the local community and the parents of its pupils . . . he/she shall be responsible for the internal organisation, management and control of the school. In carrying out his/her duties (s)he shall consult where this is appropriate with the authority, the governing body and the staff of the school.
>
> (DES, 1987, paras 2 and 3)

The purpose of this chapter is to place the appraisal of primary headteachers in the changing culture of the education system and to look at features of primary headship in the 1990s that may have to be borne in mind as appraisal systems evolve. If such systems are to fulfil their development intentions it is essential that they respond to the demands that will be placed upon schools during a period of rapid change. The issues will be dealt with in three sections: a decade of change, coping with change, and implications for appraisal.

A decade of change

The certainty of uncertainty

During the 1980s primary headteachers had to respond to the effects of a contracting education system. The consequence of falling rolls, reduced teacher mobility and an ageing teacher force together with the closure of teacher training courses and colleges have all been felt in some way by schools. During the same period, prolonged industrial action by teachers, the imposition of new conditions of service and a sometimes hostile press lowered morale within the profession.

During the late 1980s primary schools have largely emerged from the demographic trough of falling rolls though few will return to their previous numbers on roll. Having done so they have had to face the challenges associated with the introduction of the National Curriculum and the requirements of the Education Reform Act, which extended their role considerably. The poor flow of information on the National Curriculum in the initial stage generated a great deal of anxiety and uncertainty in schools. Headteachers became adept at the new skill called 'hunt the document', while their governors had access to independently mailed copies of the same.

In the face of such challenges, there was a growing realization that the changes were to be managed without the customary assumption that there would be an adequate supply of trained teachers. Headteachers also had to learn to manage their responses to change in conjunction with governors whose powers had been radically increased during the same period. Despite these factors many primary headteachers found that the introduction of a national curriculum provided them with a powerful lever for change at whole-school level. Its legislative framework had the effect of depersonalizing the change and enabling headteachers to cite implications for practice which could no longer be construed, and therefore resisted, as instances of personal preference.

Most primary headteachers would also agree that the pace of change has been too fast and that this has made the job of managing the twin concerns, of achieving goals and providing support for staff during the process of change, very difficult. Some headteachers have been unwilling to identify with the changing norms and have felt increasingly bereft of the core values that brought them into the profession. A small but significant number have taken early retirement. Others have begun the job of colonizing the legislative framework and are seeking to base their response on well articulated principles of 'good primary practice' (see, for example, an LEA's guideline, *Principles of Good Practice*; Hampshire LEA, 1989).

Handy (1989) has pointed out the disconcerting fact that contemporary change is different from that experienced before. Previously, change has often meant 'more of the same, only better'. The marked feature now is that change is *discontinuous* in its nature. In the context of schools not only is the curriculum to change, but the system for resourcing and financing educational provision is to change, the role of the LEA is to change (Audit Commission, 1989b) and in addition to all these features the inclusion of schools within the state system is already being contested.

Given the nature of such discontinuous change headteachers have, on the one hand, to convey to their staff the feeling that events are under their control rather than events controlling them. On the other hand, they must inculcate in their staff the notion that 'change is normal' and that adaptability is the name of the game. There is an obvious tension between these two requirements.

The interventionist stance of central government, the move to local management of schools and radical change or possible demise of the LEAs means that the 1990s will be characterized by the certainty of uncertainty. Schools will have to learn to live with higher levels of ambiguity while at the same time beginning to exercise new found levels of autonomy. In the 1980 the teaching profession recognized the analogy of the moving goalpost. The 1990s may well see changes in the size of the pitch and further changes in the rules of the game, such as dispensing with the concept of half time!

LMS and entrepreneurship

During the 1990s LEAs will be obliged to implement fully legislation relating to the local management of schools (LMS). By the mid-1990s all schools will be in receipt of delegated budgets managed by governors in consultation and collaboration with headteachers. Schools will become well versed in the software systems available to them as management tools. They will be accustomed to handling the full costs of teacher salaries – the most significant element in their budget. All schools, to a greater or lesser extent, will have accrued initial savings made by more efficient management of such items as energy costs, staff deployment, cleaning and caretaking, school meals and maintenance. There will continue to be budget winners and losers as the ages of staff wax and wane.

Primary headteachers and their governors will be under increasing pressure to make up any shortfall between their desired budget plan and the actual cost of meeting related needs. This gap, in the form of money or provision in kind, may be met by a range of entrepreneurial activities undertaken by or on behalf of the school. Schools differ markedly in their capacities here. For the same expenditure of time and energy, school A may raise £2,000 and school B £200 according to where they are situated. Such inequalities make it difficult to refer to an entitlement of resource levels for all pupils in the system. This moral dilemma will continue to be faced by primary headteachers during the 1990s, even granted that collaborative schemes between schools might emerge.

One effect of the stringencies of LMS is to push schools towards increased levels of entrepreneurship. Some have made part-time appointments or allocated honoraria to individuals who take on this function. This kind of activity requires resources and adds to the tasks to be managed by the headteacher. Already there are many primary schools acting in cooperation with industry and commerce to the advantage of both (e.g. Berkshire LEA, 1990). Some schools are offering a base to educational consultants in exchange for use of their services in the school. Others are marketing the expertise of individual members of staff in exchange for a fee or reciprocal service of some kind. Still more schools are paying attention to factors in the school that increase both the likelihood of attracting applicants when a vacancy occurs and the retention of staff in a situation where knowledge and experience are difficult to replace. Entrepreneurial activity is likely to increase in inverse proportion to levels of resource devolved to schools.

W(h)ither LEAs?

The full implementation of the local management of schools and the requirements of the Education Reform Act extend far beyond changes in the administrative links between schools and LEAs. In 1989 the Audit Commission commented, 'Although LEAs may have lost their empires there remains an important role for them to play' (Audit Commission, 1989b). LEAs no longer control educational institutions in their areas as they did before the Education Reform Act. Should LEAs 'fail to grasp the implications of ERA and respond positively to them they could become marginalised.' The devolution of resources to schools not only enhances their autonomy, it markedly reduces the LEAs' capacity to pursue local policies other than in limited areas. It is now central government that decides what is to be given priority. It is for LEAs to bid within this framework.

The LEAs are likely to fulfil two major functions during the 1990s: *a quality assurance* function undertaken through the process of inspection and a *service/support* function to assist schools in achieving autonomy. The Audit Commission report (Audit Commission, 1989a) recommended the shift towards more systematic monitoring and their second report (Audit Commission, 1989b) pointed out that LEAs needed to adopt 'a more structured approach to inspection and should seek to convert the results of these inspections into publicly available information on school performance' (p. 9). The responses of LEAs have differed. Some are dispensing with their advisory service and placing it on a commercial basis in a free market economy. Others have resisted the move to increased levels of inspection and seek to maintain a service function that schools may draw upon.

The changes do not simply affect the structural features of LEAs or cause redefinition of roles within them, they also have considerable implications for lay members of education committees and the functions served by such committees. Lay members have to appreciate that their direct management function has been devolved elsewhere. They have to plan more clearly and pay more attention to reviewing the performance if they are to discharge

> the quality control function envisaged for them under ERA . . .
> Their job will be even more clearly one of setting policy and monitoring progress. They will be the final arbiters of need as expressed by all various groups which form the education partnership.
>
> (Audit Commission, 1989b, p. 12)

This change of emphasis may have particular implications for the appraisal of headteachers during the 1990s. While legislative change has weakened the traditional infrastructure of the LEA, the local management of schools brings school governors nearer to the centre of the decision-making processes of the school. Indeed, in relation to key aspects of the school's work they are the prime decision-making body. Governors will engage more fully in the processes of governance if they are aided by centrally funded training. They will also be concerned with how the school is meeting the needs of its pupils and the interests of the local community. They will see the school at work, become increasingly familiar with the organization and its milieu and have the right to make and influence policy and shape decisions in the light of such knowledge. Governors are now of the school rather than outside it.

Changes in the funding of INSET will make new demands upon the management of the school. INSET funding systems changed substantially four times between 1983 and 1990 but at present LEAs submit bids mainly in relation to priority areas categorized by the DES. The bulk of such moneys will be devolved to schools and their governing bodies on an earmarked basis and will form one element in a schools budget plan. For the present, LEA INSET coordinators facilitate the process and monitor the relationship between forms of INSET provision requested by the school and the needs identified by such means as the school development plan, the school management audit, school review or some combination of these and other means of needs identification. In due course there will also be the support requirements which have been identified in the course of appraisal. The provision of LEA INSET coordinators may continue or they may disappear as schools themselves take on the role and have direct access to a devolved budget. There are already some signs that LEA INSET coordinator posts are falling victim to the need for further economies within LEAs.

The political capacity of LEAs was consistently eroded during the 1980s as a consequence of successive legislation. Should the number of schools opting for grant maintained status reach significant levels the 1990s could witness the demise of LEAs as we know them. The power of LEAs is likely to diminish anyway as schools become accustomed to the opportunities presented by delegated budgets and the principle of virement. Increases in autonomy at the level of individual schools will draw attention to the ways in which such autonomy is exercised and managed. As an LEA's power to implement policy declines the range of issues once dealt with by it will be increasingly contested at the level of the school, a situation which has considerable implications for the role of the headteacher and adds new dimensions to any appraisal of his or her work.

Coping with change

Creating external support

We have drawn attention to the changing nature of services traditionally made available to schools. One response to this situation has been the formation of networks of different kinds. Many primary schools are now collaborating with other local schools in groups known as 'clusters' as one means of developing support mechanisms in a 'grow your own' economy. The majority of primary schools prefer to cooperate rather than compete with each other, a trend wholly compatible with key values held by primary teachers. The Audit Commission (1991) noted that primary schools are beginning to approach problems more divergently through job sharing, joint-school staff appointments, sharing existing expertise and experience, joint purchasing of expensive resources and imaginative deployment of classroom assistants. All such moves widen the boundaries of schools.

Professional associations are also supporting local networks by producing informative literature on current areas of concern. Management centres and regional management consortia are producing learning support materials designed for use in networks. The 1990s will bring more sophisticated information technology systems with the same aim in mind. All these initiatives need careful management at school level. Headteachers are also likely to be out of their schools more often than in the past – as active members or constructors of networks aimed at helping them to meet new needs, as independent information gatherers, or as researchers alongside key members of staff. In Gouldner's (1957) terms primary headteachers will take on more and more features of 'cosmopolitans' as they seek to meet the emergent needs identified within their schools.

From role to task culture

We have already indicated that the role of the primary headteacher is increasing in its complexity. This has been recognized in the report on school teachers' pay and conditions (IAC, 1990), which stated

> We have been struck again this year by the heavy and increasing responsibilities falling on heads and deputies . . . the management role of heads, supported by their deputies, will be significantly enlarged as they prepare for and assume responsibility for advising their governors.

It is no longer possible for the headteacher alone to undertake all that needs to be done. Handy (1989, p. 132) has commented:

> Whereas the heroic manager of the past knew all, could do all and could solve every problem, the post heroic manager asks how every problem can be solved in a way that develops other people's capacity to handle it.

If we accept this observation then some headteachers may have to reconsider their current management style, the organizational and management structures established within their school, the patterns of provision for staff development that exist and the degree to which they delegate to others authority to act in the school. Many are adapting their practice. Some are finding it difficult or are doing so with reluctance. Others have gone further and have moved away from what Handy (1984) has called a *role culture* comprised of individual teachers with specific responsibilities towards a *task culture* in which new problems and demands are met by project teams, which are usually disbanded when a solution to the problem has been found or constructed. Such a move requires shifts in the authority structure within the school and a willingness on the part of headteachers to see their role in a different light. Smaller schools have sometimes been quickest to make such a change since many already operated as closely knit teams.

The HMI survey of primary schools (DES, 1978) found that many teachers with curriculum responsibilities were not exerting the degree of influence on practice expected of them. One explanation of this finding might well have been that differentiated roles do not fit easily into the culture of primary schools. Reciprocity rather than intervention is a more acceptable way of promoting development. The shift towards a task culture fits more easily with such norms and is more likely to engender whole-school development. It also has a significant effect on the role of headteacher.

Headship as a team task

Although the role of deputy head was established in larger primary schools in 1956 it was some considerable time before the role of deputy received significant attention by researchers, such as Coulson (1976), Waters (1979, 1983), Nias (1987) and West (1987, 1990). Different analyses have sought to show that head and deputy are seen as occupying separate roles or carrying out distinctive but complementary functions, as in Waters (1979, p. 93):

> The head must determine his own role and the tasks he feels he must carry out. Then he must consider what other matters require to be done. Some of these . . . will be allocated to the deputy, and others to different members of staff.

Head and deputy are seen as having separate job descriptions. This differentiated model is still being proposed. Henley (1989) has characterized head and deputy in terms of essential activities they each undertake.

A wholly different conceptualization of the head's and deputy's roles is expressed in a rigorous model of *partnership* in which each helps the other to develop and refine relevant skills and competences related to the management of the school. West (1990) analysed the ways in which the role of deputy was construed by practising primary heads and deputies, and found three distinct views:

- deputy as head's deputy
- deputy as prospective head
- Deputy as Deputy-head-of-this-school

The first – deputy as head's deputy – is likely to confine the actions of deputies to those which the head would have taken. It is the head's perception that dominates and the head's preferred view that prevails. In the second case – deputy as prospective head – while the deputy might be inducted into the lore of headship and made familiar with procedures etc., the stance implies an orientation to some prospective future rather than to enabling the deputy to enter significantly into accepting authority to act and contribute to the achievement of worthwhile, though complex, goals in the current school.

It is the third construction – deputy as deputy-head-of-this-school – that informs the partnership model of headship since it is committed to the present and allows deputies opportunities to exert their own identities. It is an integrated model of headship in which head and deputy share the same goals. The partnership model of headship was initially explored through the analysis of what heads and deputies:

- undertook in order to bring about their vision of the school and its work (the task dimension);
- considered to be the core skills and competences that underpinned or were brought into play in the search to achieve goals with and through other people (skills and competences).

In partnership, head and deputy are equally concerned with the achievement of goals with and through others, with what Vaill (1984) has defined as 'purposing': 'that continuous stream of actions by an organisation's formal leadership which has the effect of inducing clarity, consensus and commitment regarding the organisation's basic purpose.' Partnership in this sense goes far beyond the assumption of an agreeable social relationship. It is construed in terms of:

- shared goals (what the partnership is intended to achieve);
- awareness of values (partners may or may not have identical value systems – value positions are worked towards, not taken as given);
- action in which each develops and refines in the other the core skills, competences and arts of headship.

There is no reason why the partnership model should not be extended to include staff who may be members of the senior management team, or headship team. In this partnership model it is acknowledged that headteachers have residual accountability for what occurs in the school and are legally bound by their terms of employment. Similarly, most primary deputy heads have residual accountability for a group of pupils in their charge. This apart, the concept of partnership orientated to the acquisition and extensions of key skills, competences and arts of headship seems highly appropriate in conditions of change.

The development of skills and competences

One important aim of the partnership/headship team approach will be to focus in the job on the development of skills and competences relating to the management of the school. A means of achieving such development is through the construction of planned developmental opportunities (PDOs) by the partners concerned (case studies of PDOs can be found in West and Briault, 1990). PDOs were initially conceived as a means of promoting the development of heads and deputies but the strategy may be applied at any level within a school. The term 'planned developmental opportunity' was coined in order to emphasize that they are (a) planned and thus linked to targets with agreed criteria for success, supported by appropriate resources and sustained through a mentorship relationship between the individuals concerned; (b) developmental and therefore related to skills and competences of the individual concerned and to furthering the school's capacity to meet its stated goals; and (c) opportunistic, since development is essentially an active process in which individuals engage in self-appropriated learning. Central to such learning is the notion of critical reflection on experience. Doing and learning are seen as coterminous activities. Many of the obstacles to task achievement may thus be regarded as learning difficulties rather than as failures in oneself or others. Head and deputy or other members of the team engage in the analysis and exploration of issues and problems that have particular significance for them. Such an approach promotes joint accountability in a situation where each helps the other in the process of refining and developing relevant skills and competences that are valued by all.

Headship as a partnership can thus be construed as a relationship in which head and deputy and/or members of the headship team consciously seek to develop, each in the other, a range of skills and competences. This provides an agenda for development.

Awareness of crucial skills and competences called into play by a range of PDOs provides a reference point for critical reflection by the partnership team. But as Burgoyne (1989) has pointed out, managing is not simply the sequential exercise of discrete skills and competences. Rather, what is being worked towards through PDOs and reflection is the extension of the overall management repertoires of head, deputy and senior staff as they engage in the formal responsibilities of leading a school. Support during the course of a PDO is expressed in terms of a mentor relationship in which the capacity to engage in critical reflection on action is consistently refined. Relevant skills and competences are thus explored in use. Mentors are essentially process helpers who are not expected to proffer solutions. Developmental opportunities should reflect the notion that for learning to be significant, actions should be real in their consequences.

A partnership model of headship also requires the articulation of a vision of where the school is going and what is being worked towards in the medium and long term. This emphasizes that headship is centrally concerned with the identification and exploration of alternatives. This needs what Eisner (1979) has called the forms and functions of educational connoisseurship and educational criticism. He defines these as: '*connoisseurship* [knowing how to look, see and appreciate] and the capacity to engage in *educational criticism* [the art of disclosing the qualities of events or objects that connoisseurship perceives], (Eisner, 1979, pp. 193 and 197. These could well be called the arts of headship, for headship is centrally concerned with disclosing the qualities of educational life in a language that is understandable to a range of stakeholders. Each of these arts calls into play the conceptual, interpretative, judgemental and interpersonal competences that PDOs seek to promote.

Partnerships that consistently work towards the development of connoisseurship and educational criticism are more likely to develop the capacity to learn to live with discontinuous change that will be a feature of life in the 1990s than those that remain with traditional models. A rigorous model of headship as a management partnership provides a strategy for development that is compatible with such a culture of change.

Implications for appraisal

In previous chapters we have outlined a proposal for the appraisal of primary headteachers which has been developed in the course of our work with a number of LEAs. In this chapter we have reflected on features of the 1980s and looked forward to the 1990s. We have noted in particular the following factors:

- the discontinuous nature of contemporary change and the certainty of uncertainty;
- the emergent role of the LEA and increased levels of autonomy that will be exercised by schools;
- the effects of full implementation of LMS and the likely increase in entrepreneurship;
- the 'push' or 'pull' towards forms of collaboration and networking as a means of generating support;
- the advantages of a move towards a team/task culture and the notion of headship as a team endeavour;

- the need to develop a rigorous model of partnership that helps in the development of new skills and competences;
- the changing role of school governors.

We now consider the implications of these factors for headteacher appraisal in the 1990s in relation to three key questions: who appraises, who is appraised, and what is appraised?

Who appraises?

LEAs are currently establishing new structures and redefining their role as monitors of quality and promoters of autonomy within schools. If sufficient schools remain within the maintained system, inspectors and advisers will continue to play an important role as co-appraisers in the manner indicated in Chapter 3 and elsewhere. However, if LEAs were to be dismantled or their functions considerably reduced, then inspectors and advisers might no longer be available to perform this role. The adequacy of a single peer appraiser model might then be called into question. So what are the alternatives?

One possibility, if LEAs were to be reduced to a limited range of residual functions, might be for inspectors and advisers to be linked into the HMI system, possibly as an additional echelon, thus establishing a comprehensive approach to quality assurance and school development, including headteacher appraisal. Members of the national team (sub-divided into regions) would be available as co-appraisers and would work alongside appraiser heads on lines similar to the model already suggested in earlier chapters.

Another possibility might be to use educational consultancy services or agencies, much as LEAs and an increasing number of schools now employ consultants to assist in the planning and delivery of INSET or staff development. It would be necessary to create means of accrediting such agencies but this could possibly be done by LEAs (in whatever form they continue) or by universities, polytechnics, colleges or national bodies such as CNAA. Again, although such agencies might carry out appraisals themselves and submit reports to heads (much as management consultants do in industrial and commercial settings) it would be equally possible for a consultant employed by the agency to work alongside an appraiser head and operate along similar lines to the adviser appraiser discussed throughout this book. Clusters of schools might negotiate long-term contracts with such agencies and devise schemes (probably still within national guidelines) appropriate to their own local needs. The idea that schools might buy in independent agencies is one possibility.

Circular 12/91 provides explanation and guidance on the Regulations for school teacher appraisal. This is a normal procedural device. The Circular does not constitute an authoritative legal interpretation of the Regulations. Any contested interpretation would be a matter for the courts to decide. The Regulations concerning the involvement of a chairman of governors is far more extensive than that envisaged in the NSG report. The latter expressed 'the firm view that access to appraisal statements should be restricted to the appraisee, appraisers, the headteacher of the school, the CEO of the LEA and any LEA officer or adviser specifically designated' (para. 65). The Regulations require appraisers to provide a copy of the whole appraisal statement to their chairman of governors in addition to those mentioned earlier. The Circular softens this by adding, 'at the request of the chairman'. Appraisers are to consult with their appraisee head if they intend to collect information from governing bodies in the course of the appraisal and chairs of governors 'should have an opportunity to submit comments to appraisers designed to inform the appraisal interview'. (Circular 12/91, para. 66).

While no direct link is made between appraisal and additions to salary, headteachers may take account of information from their appraisal in advising governors on this issue. Headteachers are already in a situation where they may submit to governors as part of their budget plan, the case for additions to existing salary. It is difficult to envisage a situation where links between appraisal and pay will not be made, if only by inference.

The regulatory framework has thus ensured that headteacher appraisal is not to be the exclusive domain of professionals in the education service that headteachers might have preferred. Governors are a part of the balance and check system which has been consistently developed since the 1980 Education Act. The manner and level of governor participation in appraisal will, in part, depend upon how far and in what ways the extended role of governors has been established in their school. There is likely to be considerable variation in practice. Where the relationship between head, staff and governing body reflects collaboration and recognizes the distinction which must be made between management and governance, the involvement of governors in appraisal is likely to be innovative and productive. The scope for governor participation, at the behest of individual headteachers, remains wide and it is difficult to see how, in maintained schools, it could be extended further. In grant-maintained schools the situation is different, for here governors constitute the appraisal body and the chair has a procedural role similar to the CEO in the maintained sector.

Whilst the chair of governors may, with the agreement of the appraisee head, be allotted a significant role in the appraisal process the regular renewal of governing bodies reduces their capacity to draw upon accumulated knowledge derived from experience. There is also the problem of time given to the honorary status of their role. Nevertheless, the manner of their participation in appraisal provides one index when measuring change and development within the school system during the 1990s.

Who is appraised?

In a situation where strong forms of management partnership exist, it seems appropriate to appraise headship teams as well as, or instead of, only the head. In making this proposition, we acknowledge the legal obligations to which heads are contracted, though this might change. Headship, as distinct from headteacher appraisal, would be concerned with the appraisal of the team in terms of the roles and tasks undertaken by its members in managing the school. It would also focus upon the learning that members of the team and the team as a whole have gained, and are gaining, and how such learning is made explicit in the management of the school. It might prove helpful in this respect if members of the headship team each kept a development portfolio in which various projects, professional development opportunities or other learning experiences were recorded and possibly commented upon by other members of the team.

In many ways the appraisal of a team would be similar to that of individuals and many of the principles and approaches discussed in this book would continue to apply. Purposes would be agreed, each cycle would focus upon particular Areas and Aspects of the team's role, information would be collected according to an agreed contract and eventually an appraisal statement would be written.

The only major difference would be in the nature of the interview. A team interview is clearly an innovative idea and may require extra (group facilitation) skills on the part of the interviewers. But the benefits could be considerable as members of the team would be required to deal with issues common to them all and for which they have accepted joint responsibility. As a team building exercise it could have considerable potential.

There may be good reasons for also providing a separate interview for each member of the team to discuss his or her own professional (including personal and career) development. But such interviews need not be long compared with the full appraisal interview for a head as described in Chapter 6. Where a close partnership existed it might even be possible to deal with individual professional development in a team interview. If such were the case it would be one indicator of the organizational health of the school.

There are other possible benefits. Appraisers would have the advantage of appraising the management of the school from a range of perspectives and could potentially draw upon wider sources of information. Joint appraisal of this kind also enhances the status of deputy heads and senior staff and properly locates them in a professional development model rather than one based upon headteacher patronage, as has sometimes happened in the past.

What is appraised?

In Chapter 4 we described the Areas that constitute the management role of headteachers. They covered the management and development of teaching, learning and curriculum, staff, finance and physical resources, and external relations. These, together with professional development, including the skills and competences necessary for the management task, provide the 'menu' from which the agenda for headteacher appraisal is selected.

During a period of rapid change as described in this chapter and a growing belief that the heroic 'manager' is no longer the model of management appropriate to the 1990s, it is clear that what must be appraised will itself change. As schools take on the characteristics of autonomous, self-regulating organizations, and teams replace the solitary head, management will need to attend to the following tasks. They will need to establish a vision for the school and from it derive appropriate goals and priorities. They will set up structures and processes whereby their goals can be reached and they will seek to acquire, as a management team, the skills and competences necessary to fulfil their role. This is illustrated in Figure 9.1.

Appraisers will therefore focus upon:

1 Vision, goals and priorities. How were these established and how did the team manage the process through the support and monitoring of others?
2 Structures and processes. How were these created? Who was involved? How effective were they and what was the team's role in developing them?
3 Skills and competences. How were management development needs identified? How were opportunities created for them to be acquired by individuals and the team as a whole? How were they reviewed to ensure continuous learning by the team?

Skills and competences will cross all four Areas of headship and will

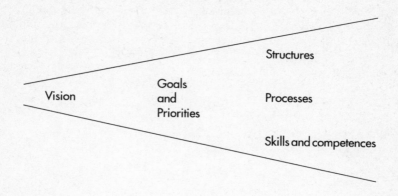

Figure 9.1 The tasks of school management.

be applied to the management and development of teaching, learning and the curriculum, staff, finance and resources and external relations. The appraisers will help the team to select Areas for appraisal and to collect information in relation to these.

The competences that are becoming increasingly valuable for managing in a 'new age' are strategic planning, policy construction and analysis, budgetary planning and control, using information technology for management information systems etc. But there are new challenges that relate to the need for marketing skills, for seeking out new opportunities, managing change, dealing with uncertainty and the stress it causes at individual and organizational level. All of these will become the joint responsibility of those who will make up headship teams in the 1990s. To appraise these will be a challenge for those who become the appraisers of the 1990s.

And henceforth?

'Change' is a word used frequently in this chapter. It will undoubtedly continue to be the byword of the 1990s. Appraisal itself is part of this change. It will be regarded by some as yet another burden that must somehow be coped with in order to meet statutory or contractual requirements. But it will also be perceived by those who have experienced a helpful appraisal as something that should become their right and their prerogative. If carried out with understanding, empathy and care it will benefit appraisees whether they be individuals or a headship team. It will provide for them the CHALLENGE, CONFIDENCE and CLARITY they seek. It may also come to be regarded as part of the overall quality assurance system that schools and the profession as a whole will wish to provide for themselves in the coming decade.

Appendix 1

Headteacher self-review form

Name _____ Date _____

It is intended that this form should be used as a stimulus and aid to your reflection upon your work. By thinking about each question carefully and writing a response you may gain new insights and perspectives.

When completed it can be used in the appraisal process in two ways. It can help you when discussing and agreeing the Areas of work that will form the focus for the appraisal. It can also be given to the appraisers, if you so wish, to provide them with more information for the interview. In any case, the last part containing questions 18 and 19 should, after completion, be returned to the appraiser head before the initial meeting.

The Areas of your work from which two will be agreed as the focus for the appraisal are the management and development of:

the curriculum;

staff;

finance and physical resources;

external relations.

In addition all appraisal interviews will include discussion of your own

Professional Development.

Remember, in all cases the appraisal is concerned with your function as a *manager or facilitator* of the above four Areas. It is not concerned with evaluating outcomes of your work but with identifying those Areas in the management of the school where developments might usefully take place. Please be as thorough and honest as you can in answering each question.

Consider the four areas of management – curriculum, staff, finance and physical resources, external relations – and answer the following questions.

1   In which of the areas are you generally satisfied with your performance?

2   Can you give reasons why this is so?

3   In which areas have you experienced difficulty and would like developments to take place?

4   Can you say why this is so?

5   Are there areas of your job which you find particularly demanding or stressful?

6   Can you give reasons for this?

7   Do you have any ideas as to how, by taking feasible action on your part, you might alleviate some of the demands or stress?

8   Your job requires management and organizing skills of a high order. How would you describe your management style?

9   Consider your relationships with the following groups and comment upon each as seems appropriate.

(a)   Teaching staff

(b)   Other staff

(c)   Governors

(d)   Parents

(e)   Pupils

(f)   Professional colleagues external to the school

10   What would you say has been the main contribution to developing the school over the past year?

11   In the light of all of the above responses, what do you see as key tasks for your own development in the coming year?

12   Is there any form of management development programme that might help you perform these tasks more effectively?

13   How would you like to see your career developing over the next few years?

14   Are there any constraints that might prevent you from reaching your career goals?

15   What new experiences, education or training might help you to achieve your career goals?

16   What steps are you taking to find such experiences, education or training?

17 During the current review process what areas involving your professional and career development would you find it most useful for the reviewers to concentrate upon?

To be returned to the appraiser head before the initial meeting

18 What is your vision for the school over the next five years? In other words, despite the constraints that you are likely to meet, how would you like the school to be in five years time?

19 Which two of the four Areas, management and development of

the curriculum

staff

finance and physical resources

external relations

do you think, at this stage, you would prefer to concentrate upon during your appraisal? Please give your reasons.

Appendix 2

Prompt list – Areas and Aspects

Each appraisal cycle should normally only deal with two out of the four broad Areas set out below, plus the 'head's own professional development'. Within each Area usually three or four Aspects should be considered. The lists below are suggestions only and are not meant to be comprehensive. There will inevitably be overlap between the four Areas.

The management and development of teaching, learning and the curriculum
Aspects

Delegation of curriculum responsibilities
Support for curriculum coordinators
Development plans
Introducing specific National Curriculum subjects
Assessment and record keeping
Availability of curriculum materials
Achieving a balanced curriculum
Monitoring the curriculum in action
Informing parents

The management and development of staff
Aspects

Interviewing and selection procedures
Induction of new staff
Role/job descriptions
Staffing structures
Decision-making procedures
Communication systems
Motivation and incentives
Discipline

Staff development policy
Identification of needs
Appraisal scheme

The management and development of finance and physical resources

Aspects

Budget planning
Capitation priorities
Spending controls
Internal allocation procedures
Fund raising
Involvement of staff
Communication with governors
Managing the school environment
Use of space

The management and development of external relations

Aspects

Public relations/marketing
The school image
Parent involvement
Governor involvement
Community support
Links with industry
Support agencies
Communications with play groups and secondary phase
Professional associations
Federations/cluster groups

Head's professional development

Aspects

General competences (applicable to each of the four Areas set out above)
    problem-solving
    communication
    decision-making
    delegation
    interpersonal skills
    planning
    time management
Future plans
    priorities for coming year
    constraints affecting performance
    career progression/development
    training needs

Remember that these are examples only and not a comprehensive list.

Appendix 3

Guidance and code of practice on the collection of information for school teacher appraisal
[Annex A of DES Circular 12/91]

1 This guidance and Code of Practice covers the collection of information for school teacher appraisal other than through classroom observation.

General principles

2 Information collection for the purpose of the appraisal of a school teacher should be designed to assist discussion in an appraisal interview having the purposes set out in paragraph 40 of the Circular.
3 Where it has been agreed that the appraisal should concentrate on specific aspects of the appraisee's job, information collection should likewise concentrate on those aspects.
4 Appraisers should act with sensitivity to all concerned and should not exhibit any bias in collecting information.
5 Those giving information should not be put under any pressure save that of relevance and accuracy.
6 General comments should be supported by specific examples.
7 Interviews for the purpose of information collection should be held on a one to one basis.
8 Any information received anonymously should not be used.
9 Information which does not relate to the professional performance of a school teacher should not be sought or accepted.
10 Appraisees should not adopt an obstructive attitude to reasonable proposals for the collection of appropriate information.

11 Neither appraisers nor appraisees should act in any way that is likely to threaten the trust and confidence on both sides upon which successful appraisal depends.

Background information

School teacher appraisal

12 The school teacher's appraiser must be familiar with relevant national and, in LEA maintained schools, LEA policies and requirements. In grant-maintained schools, the appraiser must be familiar with the policies of the school's governing body.
13 The appraiser will also need to acquire a range of background information appropriate to the appraisee's wider professional responsibilities, for example, the school's statements of aims and objectives, pastoral arrangements, equal opportunities policies, or departmental policies.
14 The appraiser should obtain copies of the school teacher's job description.

Head teacher appraisal

15 The head teacher's appraisers must be familiar with current national and, in LEA maintained schools, LEA policies and requirements with regard to curriculum, special needs, equal opportunities, staffing and cover, disciplinary and grievance procedures and other such matters relating to school management. In grant-maintained schools, the head teacher's appraisers should familiarise themselves with equivalent policies and requirements of the school's governing body.
16 They will also need a wide range of background information about the school and its context including:
— the school development plan;
— curricular policies;
— general organisation and deployment of staff;
— composition and organisation of the governing body;
— links with home, outside bodies and other schools;
— the pattern of meetings with staff and with parents;
— school activities and routines including assessment and recording systems, examination results, calendar of events;
— staff appraisal and development arrangements and arrangements for induction and probation;
— financial and management systems.
This information will need to be assembled by appraisee heads, who may provide any supplementary information they wish.
17 The appraisers should obtain copies of the head teacher's job description.

Other guidance to the appraiser

18 The appraiser should aim to agree with the appraisee at the initial meeting what information it would be appropriate to collect for the purpose of the appraisal, from what sources and by what methods.

19 When interviewing people providing information as part of an appraisal, the appraiser should explain the purpose of the interview and the way in which information will be treated.

20 Those giving information should be encouraged to make fair and considered comments which they are prepared to acknowledge and to substantiate if required.

21 Any written submissions should remain confidential to the author, the appraiser and the appraisee.

22 Those offering significantly critical comments should be asked to discuss them directly with the appraisee before they are used as appraisal information.

23 Except where personal opinion is specifically sought (for example where an appraiser is attempting to gauge staff reactions to a particular innovation), care should be taken to ensure that information is sought and presented in an objective way.

Appendix 4

Agreed Areas for appraisal

Choose three or four Aspects from two of the four broad Areas of headship indicated, plus head's own professional development. Areas of headship and chosen Aspects should be written as titles in column 1.

Area and Aspects (examples)	Agreed information gathering process		
	Appraiser to	Appraisee to	Comments
Area, e.g. management and development of staff. Aspects Staff, development policy, particular reference to: 1 Effectiveness of SD committee 2 Integration into school life 3 Views on priorities 4 Individual needs	Observe head chairing SD committee. Talk to members of committee. Interview 4 members of staff. Visit staff room and talk informally to staff as agreed.	Organize visit and times. Select staff for interview (2 involved, 2 not so involved). Arrange for committee members to talk to all staff about satisfaction of own SD needs. Arrange for questionnaire to all staff re outcome of 1990 programme. Committee to analyse responses.	Visit arranged for 1.4.91 9.00a.m. to 3.00p.m. Concentrate on views of staff on policy, their knowledge of its existence, what it contains and whether they feel involved.
Area,			

Area, professional development			

Signed _____ _____ _____ Date _____

Appendix 5

Headteacher appraisal action plan (a two-year cycle)
[Adapted from plan used by East Sussex LEA]

Appraiser action
TIME SPAN
(start to finish) 6 to 8 weeks

Appraisee action

Year 1

1 ALLOCATION

LEA allocates appraisers to appraisee and informs appraisee

2 APPRAISEE considers allocation and accepts/rejects nominated appraiser

3 APPRAISER notified of allocation

4 APPRAISER telephones APPRAISEE to establish date of initial meeting. Also telephones adviser to agree possible dates for the interview.

5 APPRAISER confirms initial meeting in writing and forwards prompt list and pro forma.

6 APPRAISEE reflects on possible areas for review using prompt list.

7 INITIAL MEETING CONTRACT AGREED

Areas and Aspects for appraisal established. Information gathering process discussed and agreed.
Dates for visits, interview and follow-up meeting agreed.

8 APPRAISER confirms interview date with adviser.

9 INFORMATION GATHERING (along agreed lines).

10 APPRAISER gathers information through documentation, observation, interviews with staff/ governors/ parents, questionnaires, and so on, as appropriate.

11 APPRAISEE gathers documentation, general information/views through discussions/ questionnaire as appropriate.

12 APPRAISER sends copy of contract to adviser.

13 APPRAISEE passes information to adviser.

14 INTERVIEW attended by APPRAISER/APPRAISEE/ADVISER Discussions cover matters initially agreed. This leads to agreed ongoing targets.

15 DRAFT COPY OF APPRAISAL STATEMENT produced.

16 FOLLOW-UP involving APPRAISER/APPRAISEE. Final wording of the STATEMENT agreed and signed. TARGETS CONFIRMED.

Year 2

1 APPRAISER contacts APPRAISEE to set up INTERIM REVIEW date.

2 APPRAISEE reflects on progress over the past twelve months on targets set at the INTERVIEW in Year 1.

3 INTERIM APPRAISAL INTERVIEW attended by APPRAISER/APPRAISEE Targets discussed and sub-targets set as appropriate.

4 DRAFT STATEMENT discussed (postal exchange might be necessary), agreed and signed. Copy sent to adviser.

References

Abbott, R., Birchenough, M, *et al.* (1989). *External Perspectives in School Based Review*. Harlow, Longman for SCDC.

ACAS (1986a). *Report on Working Groups on Appraisal/Training*. London, Advisory Conciliation and Arbitration Service.

ACAS (1986b). *Teachers' Dispute ACAS Independent Panel: Report of the Appraisal/Training Working Group*. Mimeo. London, ACAS.

Adair, J. (1983). *Effective Leadership*. Aldershot, Gower.

Adair, J. (1985). *Effective Decision Making*. Aldershot, Gower.

Adair, J. (1986). *Effective Team Building*. Aldershot, Gower.

Alexander, R. (1984). *Primary Teaching*. London, Holt, Rinehart and Winston.

Argyris, C. and Schon, D. (1974). *Theory in Practice*. London, Jossey-Bass.

Audit Commission (1989a). *Assuring Quality in Education*. London, HMSO.

Audit Commission (1989b). *Losing an Empire, Finding a Role: the LEA of the Future*. London, HMSO.

Audit Commission (1991). *Management with Primary Schools*. London, HMSO.

Auld, R. (1976). *William Tyndale Junior and Infants Schools Public Inquiry: a Report to the ILEA*. London, ILEA.

Becher, T., Eraut, M. and Knight, J. (1981). *Policies for Educational Accountability*. London, Heinemann.

Belbin, R. M. (1981). *Management Teams: Why They Succeed or Fail*. London, Heinemann.

Bennett, N., Desforges, C. *et al.* (1984). *The Quality of Pupil Learning Experiences*. Hove, Laurence Erlbaum Associates.

Berkshire LEA (1990). *Community Links across Sandhurst Primaries*. BEMAS Conference, Reading University, Berkshire LEA.

Bradley, H., Bollington, R. *et al.* (1989). *Report on the Evaluation of the School Teacher Appraisal Pilot Study.* Cambridge, Cambridge Institute of Education.

Burgoyne, J. (1989). 'Creating the managerial portfolio: building on competency approaches to management development', *Management Education and Development,* **20**, 56–61.

Butler, G. (1987). *School Appraisal in Practice.* Harlow, Longman.

Caldwell, B. and Spinks, J. (1988). *The Self Managing School.* Basingstoke, Falmer Press.

Cambridge Institute of Education (1989). *Report on the Evaluation of the School Teacher Appraisal Study.* Cambridge, Cambridge Institute of Education.

Clift, P. (1982). 'LEA schemes for school self evaluation: a critique', *Educational Research,* **24**(4), 262–71.

Clough, E., Aspinwall, K. *et al.* (eds) (1989). *Learning to Change.* Basingstoke, Falmer Press.

Coulson, A. (1976). 'Leadership functions in primary schools', *Educational Administration,* **5**, 37–49.

Cox, C. B. and Dyson, A. E. (eds) (1969). *Fight for Education: A Black Paper.* Critical Quarterly Society.

Cox, C. B. and Dyson, A. E. (eds) (1970). *Black Paper Three.* Critical Quarterly Society.

Cox, C. B. and Boyson, R. (eds) (1975). *Black Paper 1975.* J. M. Dent.

Croydon LEA (1985). *Proposals for a System of Performance Appraisal.* Croydon, Croydon LEA.

Croydon LEA (1987). *Papers Relating to Evaluation: Appraisal: Assessment.* Croydon, Croydon LEA.

Dalin, P. and Rust, V. (1983). *Can Schools Learn?* Windsor, NFER-Nelson.

Dean, J. (1986). 'Teacher appraisal: some questions to ask', *Inspection and Advice,* **22**, 1–7.

DES (1978). *Primary Education in England.* London, HMSO.

DES (1983). *Teaching Quality,* Cmnd 8836. London, HMSO.

DES (1985). *Better Schools,* Cmnd 9469. London, HMSO.

DES (1985). *Quality in Schools: Evaluation and Appraisal.* London, HMSO.

DES (1987). *School Teachers' Pay and Conditions of Employment: the Government's Proposals.* London, HMSO.

DES (1990a). *School Teacher Appraisal: the National Framework.* Draft document to all CEOs, October 1990. London, Department of Education and Science.

DES (1990b). *Teacher Appraisal: Policy and Education Support Grant,* including paper for IAC on coverage of appraisal regulations, December 1990. London, Department of Education and Science.

DES (1991a). *School Teacher Appraisal Circular 12/91 and Regulations.* London, Department of Education and Science.

DES (1991b). 'Teacher appraisal implemented by Kenneth Clarke', *The Department of Education and Science News 250/91.* London, Department of Education and Science.

Eisner, E. (1979). *The Educational Imagination.* West Drayton, Collier MacMillan.

Galton, M., Simon, B. and Croll, P. (1980). *Inside the Primary Classroom.* London, Routledge and Kegan Paul.

Gane, V. (1986). *Secondary Headteacher Appraisal: the Nub of Credibility.* Bristol, NDC.

Gouldner, A. (1957). 'Cosmopolitan and locals: towards an analysis of latent social roles', *Administrative Science Quarterly,* **2**, 281–306.

Hampshire LEA (1989). *Principles of Good Practice, a Tool for Self Evaluation.* Winchester, Hampshire LEA.

Handy, C. (1976). *Understanding Organisations.* Harmondsworth, Penguin Books.

Handy, C. (1984). *Taken for Granted? Understanding Schools as Organisations.* Harlow, Longman.

Handy, C. (1989). *The Age of Unreason.* London, Business Books.

Hellawell, D. E. (1990). 'Headteacher appraisal: relationships with the LEA and its Inspectorate', *Educational Management & Administration,* **18**(1), 3–15.

Henley, M. (1989). 'Goals, goal setting, appraisal and school improvement', *School Organisation,* **9**, 143–56.

Hersey, P. and Blanchard, K. (1977). *Management of Organisational Behaviour: Utilising Human Resources,* 3rd edition. Englewood Cliffs, NJ, Prentice-Hall.

Hewton, E. (1988a). *School Focused Staff Development.* Basingstoke, Falmer Press.

Hewton, E. (1988b). *The Appraisal Interview: an Approach to Training for Teachers and School Management.* Milton Keynes, Open University Press.

Holly, P. and Southworth, G. (1989). *The Developing School.* Basingstoke, Falmer Press.

Hopkins, D. (ed.) (1987). *Improving the Quality of Learning.* Basingstoke, Falmer Press.

IAC (1990). *Third Report of the Interim Advisory Committee on School Teachers' Pay and Conditions* Cmnd 973. London, HMSO.

ILEA (1977). *Keeping the School under Review.* London, ILEA.

King, R. (1978). *All Things Bright and Beautiful.* Chichester, John Wiley & Sons.

Kolb, D. A., Rubin, I. M. and MacIntyre, J. M. (1984). *Organizational Psychology: an Experiential Approach to Organizational Behavior.* Englewood Cliffs, NJ, Prentice-Hall.

Leithwood, K. A. and Montgomery, D. J. (1986). *The Principal Profile.* Toronto, OISE Press.

Lortie, D. C. (1975). *School Teacher: a Sociological Study.* Chicago, University of Chicago Press.

Maiden, W. B. and Harrold, R. I. (1988). 'Tools for principals to appraise their own work activities', *School Organisation,* **8**, 211–28.

MacGregor, J. (1990). 'Schoolteacher appraisal', Speech by the Secretary of State for Education to the BEMAS Conference, 14 September.

McMahon, A., Bolam, R. *et al.* (1984). *Guidelines for Review and Internal Development in Schools*. York, Longman for Schools Council.

Moore, H. (1988). 'Appraisal and the headteacher in L. Bell (ed.) *Appraising Teachers in Schools: a Practical Guide*. London, Routledge, pp. 137–53.

Mortimore, P., Sammons, P. *et al.* (1988). *School Matters*. Wells, Open Books.

Mountford, J. (1988). 'The role of critical friends in school evaluation', *School Organisation*, 8, 255–60.

Nias, J. (1987). 'One finger, one thumb: a case study, of the deputy head in a nursery/infant school', in G. Southworth (ed.) *Readings in Primary School Management*. Basingstoke, Falmer Press, pp. 30–53.

Nias, J., Southworth, G. and Yeomans, R. (1989). *Staff Relations in the Primary School: a Study of Organisational Cultures*. London, Cassell.

NSG (1989). *School Teacher Appraisal: a National Framework*. Report of the National Steering Group on the School Teacher Appraisal Pilot Study. London, HMSO.

Pyne, M. (1987). 'A primary concern', *Times Educational Supplement*, 11 December, p. xxix.

Rowland, S. (1984). *The Enquiring Classroom*. Lewes, Falmer Press.

Sallis, J. (1977). *School Managers and Governors, Taylor and After*. London, Ward Lock Educational.

Steadman, S., Abbott, R. *et al.* (1989). *Setting Standards in Schools*. Harlow, Longman for SCDC.

Suffolk LEA (1985). *Those Having Torches . . . Teacher Appraisal: a Study*. Ipswich, Suffolk Education Department.

Trethowan, D. (1987). *Appraisal and Target Setting*. London, Harper & Row.

Turner, G. (1987). 'Appraisal of a school management team', *School Organisation*, 7, 243–51.

Turner, G. and Clift, P. (1985). *First Review and Register of School and College Based Teacher Appraisal Schemes*. Milton Keynes, Open University.

Turner, G. and Clift, P. (1988). *Studies in Teacher Appraisal*. Basingstoke, Falmer Press.

Vaill, P. B. (1984). 'The purposing of high performance systems', in T. Sergiovanni and J. Corbally (eds) *Leadership and Organisational Culture*. Champaign, IL, University of Illinois Press.

Waters, D. (1979). *Management and Headship in the Primary School*. London, Ward Lock Educational.

Waters, D. (1983). *Responsibility and Promotion in the Primary School*. London, Heinemann.

West, N. F. (1987). 'Acting headship in the primary school: some management issues', *Education 3–13*, March, pp. 51–6.

West, N. F. (1990). 'Planned developmental opportunities – a strategy derived from practice', Paper given at BEMAS Annual Conference, Reading University.

West, N. F. and Briault, E. (1990). *Primary School Management: Learning from Experience*. Windsor, NFER-Nelson.

_____ *Further reading*

There is now a voluminous literature on teacher appraisal, of which the references contained in this book are only a small sample. There is much less on headteacher appraisal and much of what there is tends to be from the USA, where the sytstem is so different that examples are not always helpful. The following mainly UK references are worth perusal by those with responsibility for organizing, implementing or otherwise studying in more depth the subject of headteacher appraisal.

Bradley, H. *et al.* (1989). *Report on the Evaluation of School Teacher Appraisal Study*. Cambridge, Cambridge Institute of Education. This includes details of the six pilot projects together with comments on outcomes and issues.

Day, C., Whitaker, P. and Wren, D. (1987). *Appraisal and Professional Development in Primary Schools*. Milton Keynes, Open University. This book covers a wide range of issues closely focused on the context of primary schools and makes many references to headteachers.

DES (1990). *School Teacher Appraisal: the National Framework*. Draft document to all CEOs, October. London, Department of Education and Science.

DES (1990). *Teacher Appraisal: Policy and Education Support Grant*, including paper for IAC on coverage of appraisal regulations, December. London, Department of Education and Science.

DES (1991). *School Teacher Appraisal Circular 12/91 and Regulations*. London, Department of Education and Science. This is the formal government position embodied in Statutory Regulations in 1991. It is therefore essential reading.

Evans, A. and Tomlinson, J. (eds) (1989). *Teacher Appraisal: a Nationwide Approach*. London, Jessica Kingsley Publishers. A useful collection of papers relating to appraisal from a range of different perspectives.

Hewton, E. (1988). *The Appraisal Interview: an Approach to Training for Teachers and School Management*. Milton Keynes, Open University Press.

Montgomery, D. and Hadfield, N. (1989). *Practical Teacher Appraisal*. London, Kogan Page. Contains a useful chapter on the appraisal of headteachers.

Moore, H. (1988). 'Appraisal and the headteacher, in L. Bell (ed.) *Appraising Teachers in Schools: a Practical Guide*. London, Routledge, pp. 137–53.

NAHT (1989). *Appraisal: Head Teachers Review*. Haywards Heath, NAHT. A special edition of the *Head Teachers Review*, which focuses wholly on headteachers and deputy heads. Contains many valuable contributions.

NSG (1989). *School Teacher Appraisal: a National Framework*. Report of the National Steering Group on the School Teacher Appraisal Pilot Study. London, HMSO. Essential reading for an understanding of the present ground rules for teacher and headteacher appraisal.

Suffolk LEA (1985 and 1987). Based upon a DES sponsored project on teacher appraisal, Suffolk have produced two informative books. *Those Having Torches . . .* offers detailed information on the meaning and purpose of appraisal, schemes in operation in the UK and abroad and examples of documentation used. *In the Light of Torches* contains chapters on costs, headteacher appraisal, classroom observation and training. It also contains the full report of the ACAS Appraisal/Training Working Group, which is important reading for those following the developing situation nationally.

Trethowan, D. (1987). *Appraisal and Target Setting*. London, Harper & Row. This considers a number of matters, including the role of management, setting up an appraisal scheme, documentation, the interview, appraising the head and appraisal training. Underlying all of these is the central principle of target setting.

West, N. F. (1989). 'The professional development of headteachers: the wider view', in I. Craig (ed.) *Primary Headship in the 1990s*. Harlow, Longman, pp. 197–210. Outlines trends and demands facing primary headteachers as they enter the 1990s.

West, N. F. and Briault, E. (1990). *Primary School Management – Learning from Experience*. Windsor, NFER-Nelson. Contains examples of heads and deputies undertaking planned developmental opportunities.

Wragg, E. C. (1987). *Teacher Appraisal: a Practical Guide*. Basingstoke, Macmillan. This considers the criteria for judging teachers but gives particular attention to the place of classroom observation in the appraisal process.

Finally, each of the pilot projects has produced some material on headteacher appraisal and information on these can be obtained by writing to the LEA pilots at the following addresses:

Croydon	Project Director, Room 13, The Davidson Professional Centre, Davidson Road, Croydon CRO 6DD. Tel. 081-654 8168.
Cumbria	Project Director, Pilot Study for Teachers' Appraisal, Education Department, 5 Portland Square, Carlisle CA1 1PV. Tel. 0228 23456, ext. 2089.

Newcastle	Project Coordinator, School Teacher Appraisal Pilot Project, Kenton School, Drayton Road, Newcastle upon Tyne NE3 3RU.
Salford	Project Officer, Advisory Section, Town Hall, Bexley Square, Salford M3 5LT. Tel. 061-832 9571, ext. 341.
Somerset	Project Coordinator, Somerset Teacher Review and Development Study, Somerset Education Centre, Friarn Annexe, Wembdon Road, Bridgwater, Somerset TA6 7DL. Tel. 0278 450346.
Suffolk	Coordinator, School Teacher Appraisal Project, Room 303, County Education Office, St Andrews House, Grimwade Street, Ipswich, Suffolk IP4 1LJ. Tel. 0473 230000, ext. 4406.
National Steering Group	National Development Centre for School Management Training, 35 Berkeley Square, Bristol BS8 1JA. Tel. 0272 303030, ext. M391.

Index